GRAPHOLOGY

Patricia Marne is a journalist specialising in features and articles on graphology.

A large part of her work is in connection with personnel selection, including courses for personnel staff, and her services are also in demand for vocational guidance and marriage compatibility.

Patricia Marne started teaching graphology after studying the subject for many years. She was graphologist at the American Franklin School of Contemporary Studies in London and now teaches the subject – mainly to professional people.

Much of Patricia's work is connected with the law – her expertise is often required by solicitors and the police (in connection with anonymous letters, fraud etc.).

She has written considerably on children's handwriting and has contributed features to most of the magazines and papers in this country as well as appearing on TV and radio.

TEACH YOURSELF BOOKS

GRAPHOLOGY

Patricia Marne

TEACH YOURSELF BOOKS
Hodder and Stoughton

First printed 1980

Copyright © 1980
Patricia Marne

Published in the USA by David McKay & Co. Inc.,
750 Third Avenue, New York, NY 10017, USA.

ISBN 0 340 24792 4

Printed and bound in Great Britain for Hodder and Stoughton paper-
backs, a division of Hodder and Stoughton Ltd, Mill Road, Dunton
London, WC1B 3DP) by Richard Clay (The Chaucer Press) Ltd,
Bungay, Suffolk

Contents

PART ONE

Graphology as a Science

1 History of Graphology

Since man first started drawing on the walls of caves and then communicating by carving symbols, signs and cuneiform formations in stone, clay, and later on wood, his designs have been studied not merely for their overt message but as a guide to the writer's character and personality. Graphology, or handwriting analysis, is therefore far from new.

Its elementary principles were known six thousand years ago. The Chinese were the first to be interested in studying handwriting as a means of revealing individual traits of personality. Later, Aristotle, the philosopher and founder of literary criticism, and then Sudenonius, the Roman historian, studied the subject. The monks in the Middle Ages, too, were well practised in reading character from scripts.

The first known treatise on graphology was written by an Italian physician, Camille Baldo (or Baldi) in 1632, but it was not until the nineteenth century, that a French graphologist, J. Crepieux-Jamin, became the first to establish the basic rule of graphological analysis: that it must be studied as a whole and not as a series of unrelated symbols. In more recent years the works of Hans Jacoby, Irene Marcusse, Nadya Olanover and Klara Roman, have developed the area of knowledge so that graphology is increasingly accepted as a reliable diagnostic tool for revealing a writer's inner personality.

In the United States it is now recognised as a science, while in Europe it is an established academic subject taught at universities. In Britain scepticism still exists because it has been confused with fortune-telling, but nevertheless it is being used increasingly as a guide to better knowledge and understanding of others by business executives, psychologists and welfare workers.

The value of graphology in assessing character and personality and in giving indications of mental and physical health is obvious; in practice handwriting analysis is now helping in fields ranging from assessing personnel to giving guidance in marriage compatability, and more and more in the detection of crime where, for example, forgery is suspected.

Handwriting can be described as brainwriting, because, to the experienced graphologist, it reveals the subconscious thinking and feelings of a writer, hence the value of graphology once its basic principles have been mastered.

The only two things handwriting does not show are the age and sex of the writer. Some people are old at twenty, some still young at sixty. Many women have masculine traits, particularly if they have had a dominant role thrust upon them, and many men have feminine traits, but everyone has a mixture of both. Obviously, after analysing handwriting for a number of years, it is possible, with reasonable accuracy, to assess the writer's age group, for instance, old age will show in the deterioration of the script. There are also variations from the normal sexual patterns which show up in handwriting and these can give a clue to the sex of the writer.

Handwriting and fingerprints have one thing in common, namely, they are unique to an individual. Just as no two persons have identical fingerprints, no two persons have identical handwriting.

This book is not written for the psychologist nor for the experienced graphologist already familiar with these principles, although it may serve as a 'refresher' course. It is intended for the reader seeking an insight into this fascinating study. His newly acquired knowledge will take him into good company for he will be sharing it with Shakespeare, Sir Walter Scott, Goethe, Edgar Allan Poe and Sir Arthur Conan Doyle among a host of others.

2 The Terminology

The student of graphology today has the advantage over Shakespeare, and even Conan Doyle, because in their day there were no established scientific patterns or formulae from which to work as there are now. It is true that certain principles, based on accumulated experience, were evolved over the centuries, and these form the foundation on which scientific graphology has been built, in much the same way as other sciences have developed. There have been enormous strides forward in technical know-how, and its application, too, since Victorian days. Even the computer now plays its part in the preparation of a detailed analysis by the professional graphologist.

As with all sciences, graphology has its own terminology and techniques which can be mastered by anyone with sufficient interest and application. The temptation that comes to every student in the early stages, and which must be resisted, is to give a premature analysis on one or two aspects which he discerns without taking others into consideration.

The same handwriting can show what at first sight appear to be contradictory traits. For example, right slanted handwriting shows a socially adapted outward-going character, but there may be left-swinging underlengths showing that the writer is in fact far more introverted than he appears on the surface.

The terminology is mostly self-explanatory.

The zones: There are three zones, the upper, the middle and the lower. The upper zone is the area containing upper strokes and loops of letters such as 'b', 'd' and 'h'; the middle is the area on the line taken up by small letters such as 'a', 'c', 'e', 'm' and 'n', and the lower zone contains the lower strokes and loops of letters 'f', 'g', 'j', 'p', 'q', 'y' and 'z'.

Slant is the slope of the writing which can be to the left, upright or to the right. Often it is mixed. It shows respectively degrees of introversion, detachment and extroversion.

Form of connection in its simplest term means the way in which letters are formed and connected. It shows the writer's attitude to life, though not his total personality.

Angular, arcade, garland and thread are four of the names given to differing forms of script or lettering. Most are self-explanatory and tell a great deal about the writer.

Rhythm and regularity denote the smoothness and consistency of the writing, and according to the style of the lettering, can show anything from a cool, calm outlook to someone who is quick-tempered and butterfly-minded.

Form level is the arrangement, neatness and appearance of the script and its impact on the eye. This, too, under scrutiny is revealing.

The ABC of graphology is, of course, the knowledge of the significance of the almost countless different ways in which every letter of the alphabet, upper and lower case, can be written. At first the student may feel that this is all that really matters, and matter it certainly does, but it should be reiterated that before an analysis is made, other aspects must be taken into consideration – such as spacing between words, letters and lines, pressure, base line level, starting and ending strokes, margins, speed of writing and size.

Most people when meeting someone for the first time, whether socially or at work, form an immediate impression of them. This is dependent on appearance – what meets the eye. It is true that some people have more intuition, or psychological insight, than others, but even so everyone knows that this first impression – form level, so to speak – although important, is sometimes misleading and closer acquaintance may bring second thoughts.

This applies especially to handwriting analysis because every stroke, dot and comma tells something of the writer. One of the fascinations about studying graphology is that once armed with this technical know-how, the student will find the curtain lifting to a new understanding and perception of others.

The following pages, with essential terminology only, will enable the student to acquire, and then apply this technical know-how which, like riding a bicycle or swimming, once learned, is never really forgotten.

3 The Three Zones

A working knowledge of graphology can be acquired by anyone interested enough to study the broad principles on which it is based and then, armed with these basic concepts, the student will appreciate and welcome the finer points which follow naturally and logically. It will then be possible to make a reliable analysis. The only warning to be borne in mind is that no hasty evaluation should be made on a single trait. One of the fascinations of graphology is that there are almost endless permutations of traits in handwriting, and often many in that of the same person. To pick on one trait alone, without taking others into consideration, can result in a misleading picture.

The first basic concept is that in all handwriting – even in that as brief as a signature – there are three zones: the upper, middle and lower. (See Example 1.)

 Upper zone
Middle zone
Lower zone

Example 1

The upper is formed by loops and strokes above the line; the middle is the body or that part of the lettering on the line, and the lower, the loops or strokes which fall below the line. These indicate: first, spirituality; secondly, sociability and adaptability to everyday reality; and thirdly, primitive instincts. Ideally all three zones should balance. Where there is exaggeration of one or more it is of significance.

The upper zone reveals conscious facets such as ethical and reflective powers, the idealistic qualities of imagination, vision and religious aspirations, and philosophical and creative interests. It is linked with the super-ego (consciousness and self-criticism). It symbolises meditation, abstraction and speculation, unfettered by material considerations, and the search for perfection.

When the upper zone is exaggerated, at the expense of the other zones, there may be strong religious leanings. Full, rounded upper loops indicate imagination and emotion. Right extensions in the upper zone indicate mental activity, intellectual ambition and drive.

Lean or thin upper loops are a sign of excessive rationalisation, meanness, lack of perception and a lack of imagination.

Where there are no upper loops, the writer is logical, practical and goal-minded, with no fantasies and few spiritual interests.

The middle zone is the pivot between cultural and instinctive spheres, and symbolises the rational, socially conscious and sentimental parts of the human mind. It measures the adaptability to everyday reality and life as well as sociability and self-assurance.

Positive traits	*Negative traits*
Practical	Domineering
Realistic	Egoistical (if large middle zone)
Determined	Resentful of criticism
Strong-willed	One-track minded
Factual	Lacking vision

A small middle zone indicates that the writer may be susceptible to feelings of inferiority, only slightly emotional, matter of fact, observant and objective. It can also show intellectual and mental agility. Many men of genius write this way; Einstein is an example.

An exaggerated middle zone indicates self-centredness; the writer may be generous but thoughtless; attracted by great enterprises; anxious to impress with a tendency to exaggerate personal affairs.

Fullness indicates a wealth of feelings, affection and empathy (warmth). Leanness indicates a lack of feelings and some inhumanity. Uniformity of height indicates self-confidence and a stable disposition, but it can also indicate over-control, resulting in coldness and the exclusion of personal feelings.

Lower zone: This is the sphere of primitive instinct and basic materialism, of submerged or suppressed sexual tendencies. It indicates instinctive desires. Left extensions are a sign of introspection and of being influenced by the past.

The two letters that are significant in this zone are the small 'g' and 'y'. These are so important in graphological analysis that they are dealt with in more detail in a later chapter. (See pp. 100–113).

Size of handwriting

Handwriting that is small and even throughout shows excellent organising ability and a matter-of-fact nature with a realistic approach to life. There is sometimes a lack of enthusiasm and of flexibility in such a writer's personality, but with these are good concentration and an eye for detail.

Large writing shows plenty of self-confidence, with a love of grandeur, and indicates a certain amount of conceit and feelings of superiority in the writer. But such writers, though self-sufficient, can also be generous and chivalrous.

The line of handwriting

Writing that keeps on a straight line indicates an honest, reliable person who is unflappable and sticks to the task in hand.

If the line of writing slopes upwards, it is a sign of optimism and ambition.

If the writing slopes downwards, it means the writer is inclined to be pessimistic at times and prone to mild depression.

When the line of writing wavers upwards and downwards there is likely to be inner conflict and uncertainty.

Here again, these are finer points and are dealt with more fully later.

4 Slant of Handwriting

The second basic concept in the analysis of handwriting is that the slant reveals the writer's emotional tendency, and attitude to other people and the outside world generally. There are three slants – to the right, upright and to the left. Respectively, they represent extroversion, independence and introversion. The average slant is 30° or a little more. From 45° to 60° is excessive, while over 60° is extreme. (See Example 2.)

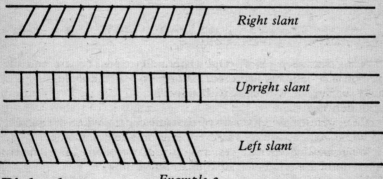

Right slant

Upright slant

Left slant

Right slant

Example 2

A slant to the right is most usual in handwriting and, when average, indicates an extroverted, outward-going personality, prepared to be friendly, often gregarious, affectionate and demonstrative. These individuals usually choose work or careers where they are in contact with their fellows. Human relationships are important to them. They comprise the larger section of the community and, dependent on other qualities, are often to be found in the area of salesmanship, acting, social and probation work. (See Examples 3 and 4.)

paper as requested) for you to sit down and write norma that its going to be care doing this at work in the

Example 3   Right slanted script

I could get out in all this g much as you do. I make the lunchtimes, when work is not

Example 4

This slant also reveals the writer's emotional nature and the importance it plays in his life. Normally, such people give and take, and are well-balanced, though human.

When the slant to the right is extreme, it can show strong emotional feelings, which are often badly controlled. (See Example 5.) The writer will be subject to the influence of others to an undesirable extent and yet display uncontrolled, irresponsible behaviour. He will be capable of strong feelings of love and hate, passion and self-sacrifice. He will lack resistance to pressures and stresses, and will be too dependent on the outside world, to whose influences he yields because of a lack of inner security and stability.

of my English Will I approve of the other

Example 5   Extreme right slant

Normal right slant	*Excessive right slant*
Spontaneous	Lacking restraint
Sociable	Lacking control
Relaxed	Impatient
Adaptable	Susceptible to influence
Enjoying human contact	Emotional
Needing communicativeness	Over-adaptable
Desires to give	Over-dependent on others
Unselfish	Self-conscious
	Poor judgment
Socially relaxed and active	Impatient
Enthusiastic	Lacking discipline
Goal-minded	Lacking common sense
Looking to future	Hasty
Altruistic	Restless
Needing variety and change	Irritable
Impulsive	Fickle
Excitable	
Has empathy	(Sometimes) violent
Enterprising	Easily distracted
Shows initiative	Thoughtless
Radical	Blind to danger
Dextrous	
Sentimental	

Upright writing

Upright writing means that the head rules the heart, and such writers are independent, cool, self-confident and not easily swayed or manipulated. They are by no means unimaginative or lacking in foresight, but they lean towards order, routine and method. Their highly developed critical sense can make them appear detached and lacking in emotional response, and leaves them vulnerable to being regarded as self-centred. When they have intelligence and ambition, they are to be found as business executives, managers or career women. They are individualistic and with the right permutation of other traits emerge as leaders and organisers. (See Examples 6, 7 and 8.)

'A dog doesn't try to give you
he just htens ...

Example 6   Upright script

good,   and   we
all   feeling   much
relaxed   and   h

Example 7

It was an ughiness fundamental and
of the abnormal nature of the Brigstoc
the principle of taste had been extra
arrangement of their home some other

Example 8

When other traits are taken into consideration, they can be seen as 'loners', cold, snobbish, aloof and egoistical.

When upright writing is seen in a child's handwriting, it shows promise of initiative and independence of manner and outlook.

Positive traits	*Negative traits*
Reliable	Indifferent
Poised	Egoistic
Cool	Rigid
Self-reliant	Lacking external interest

Independent
Controlled and restrained
Has realistic foresight
Shows personal distance
Proud
Sceptical
Self-sufficient
Able to work well on own
Calm
Has controlled feelings
Able to evaluate words
Impartial
Realistic
Has foresight
Tenacious

Lacking emotion
Unsentimental
Inhibited
Resigned
Snobbish
Detached
Cold
Self-absorbed
Pessimistic
Lacking empathy
Resigned
Secluded
Reticent
Unresponsive

Left slant

Writing that slants to the left is that of the introvert who is
latently shy and reserved. The psychologist will explain that it is
evidence of regression to childhood. Such writers are aware of the
outside world but feel isolated from it. They are conscious of their
own egos but find it difficult to relax with others and be natural. It
often appears during adolescence, partly with an awareness of sex
and sexual problems. Many such writers have had strong family
links with love and over-protection in childhood (although others
may have been deprived). The world, in contrast, seems cold, as a
result of which they adopt a cautious, and sometimes elusive
approach. They suffer disappointments and thus adopt a defensive
attitude. (See Example 9.)

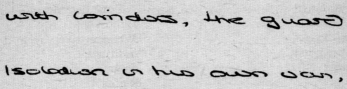

Example 9

At the same time, beneath this reserve, there can be ambition, and self-expression which finds itself in creative fields; such people maybe artists and poets. (See Example 10.)

To write . if I can get ć

you this weekend

Example 10   Left slanted script

When the left slant is extreme, it indicates repression of the emotional life, especially in girls, resulting in estrangement and detachment from the realities of the everyday world. Where there has been repression or conflict in childhood, this leads to resentment, unwillingness to adapt, and negative behaviour with resistance to environmental influence, no matter how well meant. Egocentricity leads such writers to a pose of aloofness and singularity. They are often misfits in society. (See Example 11.)

Normal left slant	*Excessive left slant*
Positive traits	*Negative traits*
Introspected	Conceited
Self-conquesting	Cynical
No illusions	Lacking naturalness
Seeking self-preservation	Narcissistic
Reserved	Self-conscious
Controlled	Arrogant
Ambitious	Egocentric
Good memory	Exaggerated self-control
Introverted	Introspective
Loyal to self	Dominated by past influences
Cautious	Repressed in emotional life
Determined	Oedipus complex
Precautious	Withdrawn
Abstracted	Over-sensitive
Independent	Inhibited
Conservative	Unapproachable
	Artificial
	Defiant

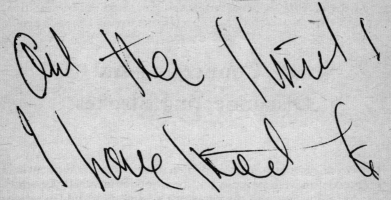

Example 11   Extreme left slant

Fluctuating slants

Fluctuating slants reveal a writer who is inconsistent, changeable, moody and emotionally unstable. He is impressionable, sensitive, easily excited but mercurial. Musicians, pop stars and dancers are frequently found to have this script. (See Examples 12 and 13.)

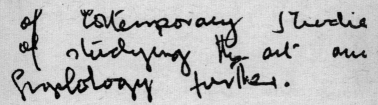

Example 12   Fluctuating slant

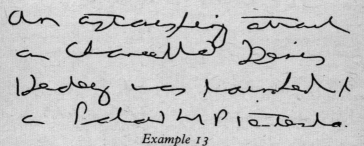

Example 13

5 Connecting and Disconnecting Strokes

Connected writing is that in which the letters are linked in a progressive movement indicating a continuous mental process with a sense of purpose and the necessary organisation and co-ordination to attain an objective. The writer is more likely to rely on logic and reason than intuition. Connected writing symbolises systematic thinking and co-operativeness. (See Examples 14, 15 and 16.)

handwriting for analysis.
second one dated 1966 is .
enclosed. I should be grate

Example 14   Connected script

have had the chance to see
of the Middle Ages and the
performed in the costumes

Example 15

saving mercy was beyond them ; they t
trumpery ornament and scrapbook art

Example 16

Disconnected script: These writers are inclined to be more individualistic and prefer to live a separate and detached life. Their
mental processes are alert and inventive. They are full of new
ideas; they can be constructively observant. They are able to think
and work alone, and may be unsociable at times. (See Examples
17 and 18.)

Jacobs, at the peak of his
broadcasting career. fell in l

Example 17 Disconnected script

Make a good job ot
so that the whole thin

Example 18

A combination of both disconnected and connected script shows
creative ability, intuition, reasoning and occasional irritation and
tension. (See Example 19.) Writers, artists, scientists and people
in the arts often write with this form of script. It belongs to the
'ideas' person who is independent, intelligent and sensitive.

He carsick dog outside the
ambiguous whether the dog

Example 19   Disconnected and connected script

6   Script Formations

For purposes of analysis, handwriting falls into a number of distinct categories. Of these the four most important are known as angular, garland, arcade and thread.

Angular

This is a disciplined movement, which expresses refusal or inability to adapt. The writer is more reliable than tolerant, and prefers firmness to compromise. He can be quarrelsome. Sometimes rigid in thinking and action, this writer is demonstrating a dominance of reason over the emotions. He can be unyielding and cold. Small, firm, angular writing indicates a steady conventional individual. (See Examples 20, 21 and 22.)

recommended in the Disc yeo and the Disc newsletter. Your

Example 20   Angular script

Thank you for your handwriting. I am very

Example 21

Looking out of the window into the garden I can see the first

Example 22

Positive traits
Capable of persistence
Reasoning rather than emotional
Strict
Conscientious
Possesses planning and
    organisational ability

Energetic
Strong minded
Has sense of obligation

Negative traits
Quarrelsome
Unsociable
Shows neurotic inner strife
Logical
Intolerant

Lacks humour
Irritable
Domineering
Suspicious
Unyielding and
    uncompromising
Egoistic

Garland

This script is soothing and effortless in appearance, and usually reveals considerable adaptability. The writer is responsive, receptive and peace-loving and will avoid arguments. He is no great hustler and may take the line of least resistance, but is warm, affectionate, kind and tolerant, preferring to follow rather than lead. Deep garlands are found in the writing of humanitarians, but they can sometimes indicate depression. (See Examples 23 and 24.)

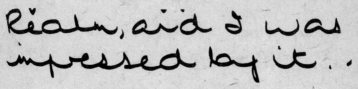

Example 23   Garland script

Postive traits
Kind-hearted
Adaptable
Natural and spontaneous
Sincere
Confident
Informal
Sympathetic and mild
Friendly

Negative traits
Submissive under challenge
Occasionally thoughtless
Fickle
Easily influenced
Lacking self-discipline
Lazy
Over-confident
Superficial
Tactless

*most important reposit
of relegious authority +
some three thousand ye*

Example 24

Arcade

Arcade script shows the writer who is rather reserved, difficult to know well, who is inclined to be formal in manner, but is innately altruistic and kind. It is the script of one who stresses form and convention, both socially and aesthetically. The higher the arcade, the more artistic the writer is likely to be. Many musicians have this form of 'm' and 'n'. The 'flat' arcade is a sign of hypocrisy. (See Example 25.)

*One point of in
may be helpful to you
say that I am at home*

Example 25   Arcade script

Positive traits	*Negative traits*
Desires to protect	Scheming
Independent	Dissembling
Trustworthy	Inscrutable
Modest	Emotionally isolated
Secretive	Morally and socially
	bigoted
Deep feelings	
Proud	
Balanced	
Diplomatic	

Thread

Thread writers are opportunists, able to manipulate situations to get their own way. They are usually versatile and spontaneous, with intuition and perception. They are often creative to their own advantage, and not over-scrupulous. They can be deceitful and have no high regard for established conventions, and are clever and intelligent. Creative people, outstanding in their chosen field, often have thread writing. (See Example 26.)

Example 26   Thread script

Positive traits	*Negative traits*
Mentally alert	Lacking stamina
Adaptable	Easily influenced
Talented	Elusive
Diplomatic	Lacking conscience
Intelligent (with perception and intuition)	Resentful
Disregarding established forms of conventionality	Rebellious against authority
Instinctive	Insincere
Perceptive outlook	
Psychologically talented	

Copybook script

Sometimes this type of script serves as a mask. It is often the writing of petty criminals, and is a sign of immaturity, dullness and stupidity. It must not be confused with the copybook script of children. (See Example 27.)

usually starts wit

ational and neurot

be extremely thin

Example 27   Copybook script

walks in beauty like the night,
cloudless climes and starry skies,
all that's best in dark and bright
it in her aspect and her eyes.

Example 28   Mirror writing

Mirror writing

Mirror writing is writing that has been written from left to right and the letters reversed. With children it is not uncommon, and corrects itself. It is sometimes found in the handwriting of handicapped people. In the writing of an individual not handicapped, it can reveal mental disturbance of a severe nature. (See Example 28.)

Wavy line

This is often found in fast writing and indicates an intelligent and energetic personality. It also demonstrates an ability to adapt to circumstances and diplomacy. There is a tendency to avoid decisions and a lack of firmness. (See Example 29.)

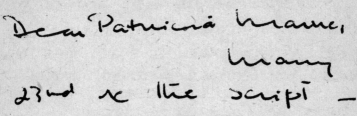

Example 29   Wavy line

Sacré Coeur

This is taught in some French schools and is used by members of certain social level groups especially in Catholic countries. It is artificial writing which indicates a subdued individuality, insincerity, inhibition and masks hypocrisy and a tendency to hush things up. (See Example 30.)

Example 30   Sacré Coeur

PART TWO

Ten Basic Clues in Graphology

1 General Layout of Script

A well arranged script is legible, the margins are normal and the spacing between the lines and words is even, consistent and pleasing to the eye. It indicates an ability for organisation and co-ordination. Intellectually it is evidence of a wide mental range, clarity of judgment and following the head rather than the heart, putting brain before natural instincts and spontaneity.

Accompanied by regular rhythmic balance, it shows clear-mindedness, orderliness, intelligence, power of elucidation, executive skill, abstract thinking, a cultured mind with discernment and a constructively critical approach. It shows a born organiser. (See Example 31.)

causes anomalies and has a signifi
If the retirement age were to be equal
benefit could increase very significant

Example 31   Well arranged script

Here are brief analyses of different forms of layout:

Badly arranged: This indicates that the writer does not plan ahead or make preparations. He has no appreciation of time, is spontaneous but indecisive, and has no sense of economy generally. (See Example 32.)

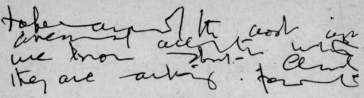

Example 32   Badly arranged script

Clear spacing: Shows an orderly mind; conversely, chaotic spacing shows erratic thinking and behaviour.

All round liberal: Means self-assurance and expansiveness.

Large spacing: This shows isolation and detachment from social relationships and lack of spontaneity.

Extremely large spacing: Can mean intellectual pride, and snobbery leading to melancholia.

2 Form Level

Form level is the general appearance of a script, and it is from this that the first impresssion of the writing as a whole is gathered. The naturalness or artificiality of the writing, the way the letters are formed, distributed, and the type of script combine to give form levels.

Harmony and well-balanced spacing mean that the writer is able to plan and organise and has an uncluttered mind.

If the script flows with good spacing between the lines and the words, it indicates a quick intelligence, and if the writing is small, intellectual maturity. (See Example 33.)

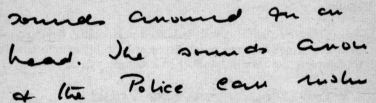

Example 33   High form level script

Laborious writing with artificial flourishes and embellishments, irregular spacing, and painstaking copybook style with large writing, indicate a desire to 'show off' and intellectual inferiority. (See Example 34.)

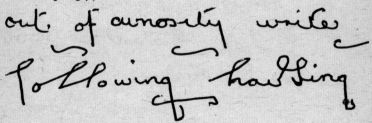

Example 34   Laborious script with artificial flourishes

3 Base Line

The base line is the line on which the letters are written, and because this line reveals the emotions and feelings of the writer, as well as his mental state, it is especially significant in handwriting analysis.

The writing can vary considerably, depending on fatigue, depression, illness, optimism, ambition, pessimism or elation. It may be straight, wavy, ascending, descending, erratic, or constant and stable.

Straight even baseline: A well-balanced personality, having a sense of direction, self-control, reliability, and an ability to maintain drive to complete the task in hand. (See Example 35.)

Example 35   Straight even base line

Example 36

Undulating: This indicates unreliability, indecision, (if thready) and an inclination to avoid commitment. The writer lacks stability and can be crafty, impressionable and over-sensitive. He has a feeling of insecurity. (See Examples 36 and 37.)

Example 37   Fluctuating base line

Convex: This means the writer is volatile, is readily enthusiastic but lacks persistence and is subject to periods of elation, alternating with sinking spirits.

Concave: This too shows the writer to be volatile and subject to varying moods, but he has the ability to fight against pessimism and to stick things out.

Extremely variable: The writer is hyper-sensitive and moody.

Ascending: This indicates optimism, and a person who is excitable, enthusiastic, increasingly active, impulsive, ambitious, gregarious and a fighter.

With no right margin: The writer is thoughtless but courageous.

Descending: This shows depression, pessimism, criticism, and despondency which may be due to ill health, tiredness or weakness.

Line ending compressed: This is evidence of a time waster, and a person who is improvident, lacking foresight and organising ability.

Downward stepped line: This is where the lettering descends in steps. It shows a writer fighting against weariness supported by strong feelings of responsibility.

Upward stepped lines: Attempts to put brake on impulsiveness that asserts itself.

Broken line: Incoherent thought and action.

Writing above printed line: Lacking sense of reality and possibly enthusiastic for independence.

Below base line: Strong sense of reality, but devoid of enthusiasm, concerned with material things.

4 Regularity and Rhythm

Regularity and rhythm, speed and pressure together indicate the energy, drive and versatility of the writer. These features are important for judging his attitude to work and achievement or failure.

A regular script is when the size of small letters, the slant, the spacing and the loops and strokes are constant.

Rhythmic writing is a regular script which is consistent throughout, flows effortlessly and has a harmonious appearance. (See Example 38.)

Example 38   Rhythmic script

A regular script reveals self-control, harmony, self-discipline, will-power, ability to concentrate, singularity of purpose and a sense of duty.

Rigid regularity, without rhythm, indicates strong self-discipline and suppression of the personality. Often the writer shows low emotional responses, and is colourless and dull.

Regularity, but with insufficient spacing, is a sign of a neurotic disposition.

An irregular script shows an emotional and spontaneous writer who has sensitivity, liveliness, is not bound by tradition, will take days off from work, is absent-minded and lacks persistence and application.

Unrhythmic script indicates a high degree of emotionalism, abrupt changes of temper, and a writer who is 'nervy'. (See Example 39.)

Example 39   Unrhythmic script

Uneven, unrhythmic script: If this writing has varying intervals between words, lines or letters, and the pressure slant and size of letters also vary, this reveals restlessness, excitability and a lack of harmony and balance.

5 Size of Script

The size of script reflects the size of personal self-esteem or ego of the writer, except in the case of royalty, nobility and a national leader whose official signature must be distinctive.

Medium and normal: Balanced writing belongs to a person who is neither over-confident nor under-estimates himself. He usually conforms to normal conventional standards.

Large: Large handwriting indicates that the writer is subjective rather than objective. (See Examples 40 and 41.)

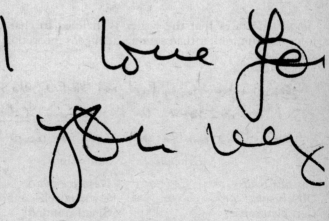

Example 40 Large script

Example 41

Positive traits	Negative traits
Accepts a challenge	Lacks objectivity
Needs recognition and attention	Undisciplined
Self-confident	Inconsiderate
Proud	Immodest
Optimistic	Meglomaniacal
Generous	Absentminded
Bold	Tactless
Spendthrift	Careless with money
Loves luxury	Boastful
	Tends to be a poseur
	Lacks accuracy
	Ignores realities

Small: Indicates that the writer is inclined to channel energies into thinking, rather than action; intelligent theoretical mind. (See Example 42.)

Example 42   Small script

Positive traits	Negative traits
Observance	Lacking self-confidence
Conscientious	Small-minded
Realist	Inferiority complex

Concentrated
Tolerant
Reserved
Power to assimilate
Business acumen
Thoughtful
Studious
Modest
Strongly inclined for detail
Executive ability
Critically minded

Resigned
Pedantic
Over-scrupulous
Economy of mind
Hypochondriac
Submissive

Wide Script

Normal script is when the distance between the downstrokes is equal to the height of small letters. Very precise and consistent distance shows a strong conscious will. Wide writing is normally spontaneous and indicates emotional adjustment to everyday life. The amount of space taken shows naturalness and free emotion. It often goes with a right slant. It is usually formed by arcs, slopes and circles covering plenty of space, rather than angles or angular writing. (See Example 43.)

Example 43   Wide script

Wide script with heavy pressure: This shows expansiveness and independence, preference for large spaces to live and work in; ambition, outspokenness, lack of tact, lack of restraint, egoism, vanity, pride, imagination, with a tendency to wander from the point and a lack of clear reasoning or perception.

Wide with left slant: Indicates strong social sense but limited by suspicion; the writer is likely to show caution with a degree of cunning. (See Example 44.)

*I wonder if you cou
me with my problem
I have Aubran Rai*

Example 44   *Wide with left slant*

Wide with light pressure: Indicates carelessness, extravagance, inability to regulate and control feelings, seeking attention and admiration. Can be over-sensitive and highly strung under emotional tension.

Excessively wide: Shows an inconsiderate, extravagant, impressionable, imaginative person who has difficulty in controlling feelings. (See Example 45.)

*by   no party line,
It is the   total
and the   right*

Example 45   *Excessively wide*

Wide upper loops: Indicates imagination, ability to visualise and good perception.

Wide middle zone: Shows emotional warmth, sociability and a genial, cheerful disposition.

Wide lower loops: These are signs of exaggerated emotion, over-imagination with leaning towards fantasy and emotional daydreaming with sexual overtones. Long loops indicate dreams of materialistic values, sexual and money matters.

Narrow Script

Narrow script is an indication of insecurity and of an unsure ego. The writer is probably reserved, matter-of-fact, lacking in warmth and is indifferent to others although sometimes he may crave for company. He can be clear-minded but may be short of tact or imagination.
Here are examples:

Narrow with heavy pressure: Inhibited, over-cautious, self-disciplined, economical, anxious. (See Example 46.)

Narrow with light pressure: Timid, modest, fears life and distrusts others. Inhibited to the point of being neurotic. (See Example 47.)

Very narrow letters: Anxious or obsessional state, inner conflict.

Example 46   Narrow with heavy pressure

Example 47   Narrow with light pressure

Narrow upper zone: Abstract thinking, analytical, ascetic, sober, critical sense. (See Example 48.)

*please analyse my handwriting
for me.*

Example 48   Narrow upper zone

Narrow middle zone: Cold, lacks generosity and feelings towards other people and has no inner resources.

Narrow lower zone: Concentrates on material and instinctive side but directed to reality rather than emotional satisfaction.

Extremely narrow: Emotionally cold, instincts stunted, austere sense of duty.

6 Speed

The basic speed of handwriting is set by the writer's nervous system. The writer who has more experience of using a pen is obviously speedier than anyone less familiar with pen or pencil. Speed and clarity reveal whether reactions are fast or slow in thought or action. Such script demonstrates the depth of emotional and social responses and shows an intellectual grasp of things, situations and people.

It is indicated by fluency. The small 'i's are dotted and 't's are crossed to the right. There are no starting strokes and writing usually extends to the right, is connected, garland or thread with small script and original letter formations (See Example 49.)

Example 49 Fast script

Fast writing

Positive traits	*Negative traits*
Tends towards extroversion	Poor concentration
Adaptable	Lacks analytical approach
Quick mental grasp	Excitable
Objective	Rash
Needs stimulation	Unreliable
Enthusiastic	Hasty in decision

Energetic and vital	Aimless
Impulsive	Shallow
Rapidly adjusts to new situations	Too susceptible to influence
	Lacks planning ability

Excessively hurried: Indicates blind zeal and rashness without thought of the consequences. The writer may be nervous, pathologically impetuous and slapdash.

Slow writing

This is generally disconnected copybook form level and is a painstaking legible script, with the letters 'i' and 't' carefully dotted and crossed and is uniform. (See Example 50.)

yes, I do think some people: smoking to impress others

Example 50   Slow script

Positive traits	*Negative traits*
Steady	Passive
Thrifty	Over-cautious
Careful	Lazy
Wary	Has moods of anxiety
Neat	Mentally slow
Prudent	Self-conscious
	Weak-willed
	Gullible
	Inhibited
	Semi-literate

If the pressure is weak, it may signify apathy and indecisiveness, and if with slurs and pasty strokes, the writer is calculating, sensual and not always honest or reliable.

7   Pressure

The choice of nib or pen influences the pressure, and writing with a ball point script should be studied through a magnifying glass to gauge the degree of pressure. Strong writing does not necessarily indicate a violent nature but accumulated energy and drive. The pressure is usually heaviest in the down strokes.

Heavy pressure (See Example 51.)

Positive traits	*Negative traits*
Tenacious	Vain and conceited
Conscientious	Stubborn
Strong willpower	Obstinate
Determined	Irritable
Self-controlled	Aggressive
Energetic and vital	Brutal
Fearless	Repressed
Prefers direct action	Impulsive
Forceful in argument	Sensuous
	Fearful

Example 51   Heavy pressure

Heavy pressure with regular writing: Willpower, independence, efficiency, perseverance, self-will and capacity for action.

With slow script: Suppressed energy with lack of self-control, leading to violent reactions.

Medium pressure: The majority of writers fall into this group and the pressure can vary. Other considerations must be taken into account for an analysis. (See Examples 52 and 53.)

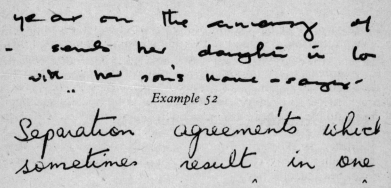

Example 52

Separation agreements which sometimes result in one

Example 53   Medium pressure

Light pressure: This is a sign of sensitivity. If the pressure is extremely weak it could reveal physical weakness and lack of energy and enthusiasm, as with maladjusted delinquents. (See Example 54.)

Positive traits	Negative traits
Feminine	Lacking initiative
Flexible	Lacking vitality
Sympathetic in understanding	Lacking resistance
Alert (spiritually and mentally)	Yields under pressure
Energetic mentally (not physically)	Weak-willed
Susceptible to atmosphere	Irritable
Modest	Easily offended
Agile	Unreliable
	Superficial
	Touchy

is, I suspect, a very n form of analysis than p it is for this reason

Example 54   Light pressure

Pasty script: This has up and downstrokes of equal thickness and is very often found in the handwriting of people who rely on their senses. They are down to earth and happier when close to nature (e.g. gardeners or farmers). They are sensitive to colour and are good artists. Very thick strokes show sensuousness, strong sexual urges, lack of spirituality, lack of discipline and easygoing manners, susceptibility to temptation and good living. Some people with such writing are brutal, crude and indulge themselves to excess.

Smeary, and possibly disorganised strokes show laziness, irresponsibility, 'shady' character, addiction, lack of moral discrimination. (See Example 55.)

not that you would know that the looks at

Example 55   Pasty script

Sharp script: This has light pressure but still with a difference in up and down strokes, the pen very often being held tightly at a more upright angle. This is often seen in the writing of lawyers, critics, surgeons and master-craftsmen. It shows restraint, reserve and critical understanding. Such writers are self-disciplined and follow their heads rather than their hearts. They do not gain full enjoyment out of life because of their scepticism but they are moral and high principled. They can be touchy.

If the script is very sharp it shows aggression, egoism, querulousness and lack of kindliness. (See Example 56.)

Basque gunmen marked the third death yesterday by shooting the attack. Three cars drove past

Example 56   Sharp script

8 Margins

Margins, according to size, show the writer's aesthetic sense, balanced generosity, meanness, sense of humour, sense of values and his attitude to the past and the future.

The left margin represents the past and its influences, both emotional and environmental, while the right margin represents the future and any forward looking goal the writer may have. A discrepancy between the two may sometimes be a sign of conflict.

The person who has an urge to fill up all his margins and empty spaces does not know when to make a clean break, and possibly practises over-economy.

Left margin

This reveals reserve, or lack of it, social background (often a hereditary link) and pride, refinement, generosity or thrift.

Wide left margin: This means a cultured background, a liking for lavish living, sometimes snobbishness, reserve, disinclination to mix, and it can show a desire to keep the world at bay.

Narrow left margin: Informality, desire for popularity, thriftiness, limited family background, desire for secure life, tendency or necessity for economy of time and money, even meanness, lack of good taste, no tact: may have poor educational background.

Convex left margin: Initial formality and generosity reduced and natural thriftiness reasserted.

Concave left margin: Intended thrift not maintained but may be resumed.

Right margin

Wide right margin: Fear of the future, difficulty in coping with personal problems, extravagant, reserved, self-conscious.

Narrow right margin: Communicative, hasty, vital, uninhibited, not apprehensive about future, sometimes sceptical and suspicious.

Irregular right margin: Shows a desire to travel, adventurous spirit, but lacking in consistency.

Upper margins

Wide: This is a sign of formality and a desire for others to take the initiative, a lack of self-confidence and a certain amount of modesty or snobbishness.

Narrow upper margin: An indication of economy; and could be lack of education.

Bottom margin

Wide bottom margin: Shows fear of emotion, over-concern with the sexual and instinctive drives and apprehension about sex.

Narrow bottom margin: Materialism, sensuality and emphasis on the physical.

No margins

Can mean compulsive thrift bordering on stinginess.

Very wide margins all round

Shows phobia or fear, a feeling of isolation, representing a wall round the writer keeping him safe and secretive. The writer has no desire for social intercourse and has an inclination to snobbishness.

9   Spacing between Words and Lines

Spacing between words and lines shows the writer's sociability and adaptability and indicates his or her attitude towards people.

A good organiser will have clean, well-balanced spacing, demonstrating an orderly mind. (See Example 57.)

vichaller, whon the soldiers

the harbour in the hope the

Example 57   Well balanced spacing

If the spacing is muddled and cramped, it shows a lack of reserve and impulsiveness, an unmethodical mind, emotional instability and often weak will. (See Example 58.)

Example 58   Spacing muddled and cramped

Generous spaces between words indicate discrimination, taste, culture and an objective mind. If too large, it shows isolation and extravagance. (See Example 59.)

I'll see you

Dont forget to ask

Class can come in

Example 59   Wide spacing shows generosity

Small spaces between words show that the writer needs to be with people, and can only function when surrounded by them. It indicates a lack of objectivity and intolerance; if too small it shows thriftiness bordering on meanness. (See Example 60.)

4. Your Disc cash card must after goods or service has

Example 60

Spacing between words

Wide: Often seen in adolescence. If seen in adults it shows those critical of other people, conceited, isolated, reserved, lonely, cautious and inhibited. (See Example 61.)

can   see   you   to

can,   but   I   will   not   y

Example 61

·*Narrow*: Impelled by direct action rather than by consideration and reasoning. Action, lack of reserve, impatience, self-contained units generating immediate power and action.

Irregular: Gullible, may be emotionally unstable or immature.

Letters overlapping: Unchecked impulses, identification with other people's reactions.

Generous spacing: May be wasteful of time, money or emotion; generally extravagant.

Over-large: Indicates isolation. (See Example 62).

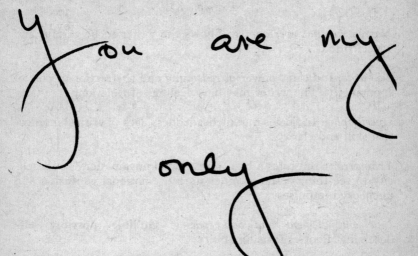

Example 62

Spacing between lines

Spacing shows the state of mind – orderly or erratic – and should be accompanied by rhythmic balance. If all round spacing is clear, it shows orderliness, power to elucidate, executive skill, abstract thinking, intellectual thinking and culture, surveying qualities, discerning and critical faculties.

Irregular: Not always successful in intellectual endeavours due to lack of application and erratic behaviour.

Equal distance: Shows clear and mature thinking, assimilates emotional experiences and maintains integrity. (See Example 63.)

might have been prizes for the blind.
astray over carpets and curtains ; then
instinct for disaster , and were so curve

Example 63

Narrow but not overlapping: Shows the writer to be careful and conscientious.

Too wide: Indicates power of reasoning and abstraction at cost of spontaneity. The writer may have feelings of isolation.

Overlapping: Indicates muddleheadedness, lack of critical intellectual skill and clarity.

Too narrow: Indicates a highly developed imagination, an incapacity to see things clearly, inner unrest, emotional confusion and unchecked impulses.

Line entanglement and bad spacing: Gullible, possibly self-deceiving. Poor organising ability.

Insufficient spacing between lines but large between words: Clarity only for short distances.

Few lines on page, over-large spacing: Indicates detachment from social or psychological relationships, lack of spontaneity, extreme pride and snobbery, can also lead to a melancholic state through isolation.

10   Starting and Ending Strokes

Starting strokes

Long starting or beginning strokes show the writer who likes to make preparation, but who can waste time and effort before getting down to things.

Starting strokes have many forms; they can be rigid, short, long, hooked, wavy, even circled or clawlike.

If they are stiff they show narrow-mindedness, rigidity of belief in conventional ideas and a closed mind to new ideas.

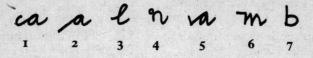

1	Hooked starting strokes:	Aggressive, persistent, tenacious
2	Starting from lower zone:	Quarrelsome
3	Wavy line:	Has sense of humour
4	Small circle:	Jealous
5	Ticklike stroke:	Has a temper
6	Claw:	Money minded
7	No starting stroke:	Indicates a practical person who grasps a situation quickly and gets down to things promptly

Ending strokes

Long ending strokes demonstrate the writer who cannot finish things cleanly but hangs on, like the caller on the phone who takes five minutes to say goodbye; they also denote caution and self-protection. Very often such writers will add a stroke at the end of the line keeping the space occupied so that no one may 'jump' in. The ending of the small 'e' is of special importance.

Here are some interpretations:

1	Upward stroke to right:	Altruistic
2	Tick-like stroke:	Quick thinking
3	Ending abruptly at the base:	Selfish, inconsiderate
4	High in air:	Exhibitionistic
5	Thick, heavy, descending:	Brutal
6	Exaggerated base horizontal:	Worries, cannot let go personal habits
7	Curling over to left:	Introverted, guilty
8	Angular:	Aggressive
9	Hooked:	Deceitful
10	Left and covering word:	Secretive
11	Looped:	Eccentric, dishonest
12	With sudden pressure:	Tense, aggressive

Small 'e' ending strokes have a special significance:

1	Normal rounded:	Normal friendly relations
2	Long terminal stroke:	Generous
3	Hook at end:	Stubborn
4	High in air:	Dreamy, may have interest in occult
5	Abrupt final:	Reticent, ends friendships abruptly
6	Rigid end stroke down:	Dominant, egoistic
7	Greek:	Cultured
8	Filled in:	Sensual
9	Long down stroke:	Intolerant (if heavy pressure: brutal)
10	Left under stroke:	Selfish, cautious
11	Curled over above:	Protective streak
12	Long hook on ending stroke:	Tenacious

PART THREE

The ABC of Graphology

1   Capital Letters

The capital letters in graphology reflect the writer's evaluation of himself.

When not abnormally large or small, but balanced in relation to the rest of the script, they are described as average and have no especial separate significance.

Large: When the capitals are unusually large, they show ambition, pride, a high regard for position and status, vanity, love of display and a tendency for showing off. The writer has feelings of grandeur, and a desire to be recognised as important, but often has an inferiority complex. (See Examples 64 and 65.)

Example 64

Example 65

Small: Capitals when small in relation to the rest of the script show concentration, reserve, lack of self-confidence, over-scrupulousness, economy, power to assimilate facts, love of detail, conscientiousness and modesty.

Narrow: Capitals which are narrow, indicate shyness, reserve, and sometimes thriftiness amounting to meanness.

Broad and wide: Such capitals show self-conceit, arrogance and impertinence.

When capitals are vertical and followed by right slanted letters, it means the writer may be cautious but can overcome initial inhibition.

Not connected: Capitals not connected with the letters that follow, show intuition and a person who plays hunches. (See Example 66.)

Poor vichuals at high rise to much discontent caused the serious muhi in 1588. Yet in this case

Example 66

Different style: Capitals different in style from the rest of the letters show that the writer is creative and versatile, but likes to be independent and is unreliable.

Bizarre capitals: These are evidence of an eccentric or affected personality. (See Example 67.)

On the question of st. literary tastes, mai

Example 67

Simplified: Capitals without embellishments show creativity, objectivity, maturity, interest in cultural pursuits, a direct approach, and, if the script is angular, the writer has a ruthless streak. In low level handwriting they can show an inferiority complex. (See Example 68.)

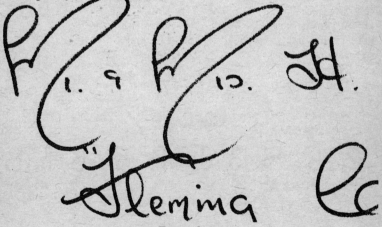

Example 68

Touched up: Touched up capitals show a neurotic type of personality, who is excessively sensitive and possibly suffers hypochondria. Sometimes this can happen in what are known as 'motive' words such as God, sex, death and mother, which are often written with pressure because such words cause the writer to react with anger, fear, or apprehension.

Printed capitals: Indicate interest in literary matters and familiarity with the printed word, reading and writing.

Exaggerated embellishments or loops: Indicate pomposity, but can come from mental illness, hallucinations or megalomania. (See Example 69.)

Example 69

Here are the varying significances shown by the letters of the alphabet:

Capital A

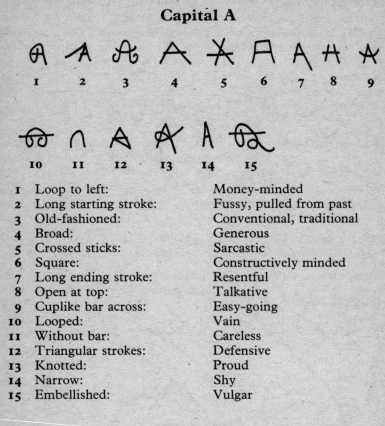

1	Loop to left:	Money-minded
2	Long starting stroke:	Fussy, pulled from past
3	Old-fashioned:	Conventional, traditional
4	Broad:	Generous
5	Crossed sticks:	Sarcastic
6	Square:	Constructively minded
7	Long ending stroke:	Resentful
8	Open at top:	Talkative
9	Cuplike bar across:	Easy-going
10	Looped:	Vain
11	Without bar:	Careless
12	Triangular strokes:	Defensive
13	Knotted:	Proud
14	Narrow:	Shy
15	Embellished:	Vulgar

Capital B

1	Full and round:	Egoistical, also generous
2	Large bulb at top:	Cautious
3	Large bulb at bottom:	Gullible
4	Like number 13:	Familiar with figures
5	Flourished:	Fussy, show-off
6	Open at bottom:	Talkative
7	Enrolled:	Egoistical
8	Stroke at top extended:	Enterprising
9	Narrow:	Shy
10	Printed:	Literate
11	Square shaped:	Constructively minded
12	Peculiar shape:	Erotic sexual symbolism
13	Round and extra large:	Emotional

Capital C

1	Enrolled with loops at top and bottom:	Crafty, deceitful
2	Round and full:	Idealistic, kind
3	Angular:	Aggressive, quick-minded
4	Arc-like:	Ambitious
5	With claw:	Money-minded
6	Scythe-like:	Sarcastic, resentful
7	Enrolled at bottom:	Egoistic
8	Black spot:	Has past problems
9	Square:	Aggressive

Capital D

1	End stroke going back:	Egoistic
2	Open at bottom:	Gossipy

3	Claw:	Greedy
4	Embellished:	Show-off
5	Flying loop at top:	Dreamer
6	Angular:	Constructively minded
7	Open at top:	Talkative

Capital E

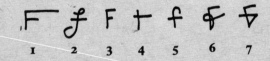

1	Stroke underlining word:	Self-admiring, vain
2	Two arcs:	Very quick-minded
3	Enrolled:	Greedy
4	Block letter:	Cultured
5	Tall and narrow:	Inhibited
6	Rounded:	Warm personality
7	Middle stroke extended:	Cautious
8	Flourished:	Vulgar
9	Overstroked:	Neurotic

Capital F

1	Stroke extended over whole word:	Patronising, protective
2	Flowing:	Sensitive, artistic
3	Printed:	Literary interest
4	Cross-like:	Fatalistic
5	Loop at top:	Dreamer
6	Knotted in middle:	Cautious
7	Angular triangular loop:	Emotionally disappointed

Capital G

1	2	3	4	5	6

1 Claw to left: Avoiding responsibility
2 Large upper loop: Dreamer
3 Like figure 8:   Acquainted with literary work
4 Large bottom loop: Exaggerated ego
5 Triangular loop: Sexually disappointed
6 Printed: Reader

Capital H

1	2	3	4	5	6

1 Narrow: Reserved
2 Broad: Extravagant
3 Block letter: Reader
4 Elaborate: Lacking taste, vulgar
5 Tall and thin: Inhibited
6 Involved cross bar: Able to get out of situations

Capital I

(See p. 82)

Capital K

1	2	3	4	5	6	7	8

1	Arc to left:	Antagonistic
2	Disconnected letter:	Many ideas but poor organiser
3	Knotted:	Capable, thorough
4	Stroke extended under line:	Defensive, uncompromising
5	Tentlike:	Aggressive
6	Enrolled:	Egoistic
7	Like Capital R:	Eccentric
8	Second stroke short:	Ambitious

Capital L

1   2   3   4

1	Looped to left:	Vain
2	Enrolled:	Insincere, greedy
3	Long starting stroke:	Argumentative
4	Pound or dollar sign:	Money-motivated

Capital M

1   2   3   4   5   6   7   8   9   10

11   12   13

1	Arcade shape:	Tactful
2	Broad:	Wasteful, extravagant
3	Narrow:	Inhibited, mean
4	First stroke high:	Egoistic
5	Second stroke high:	Seeks approval

6   Large loop left: Professionally jealous
7   Small loop left: Personally jealous
8   End stroke below baseline: Dislikes compromise
9   Old fashioned: Conventional
10 Angular top: Impatient
11 Ornamented: Vulgar
12 Turned inwards right: Defensive
13 Printed: Cultured

Capital N

1   Narrow: Inhibited
2   Last stroke extended: Enterprising
3   Starting with small loop: Jealous (of one person)
4   Stroke over entire word: Patronising
5   Large circle: Jealous (professionally)

Capital O

1   Open at top: Frank, friendly, talkative
2   Simple: Unpretentious
3   Enrolled: Secretive, deceitful
4   Very large and broad: Show-off
5   In zero form: Aptitude for figures
6   Large knot: Tricky, can be secretive
7   Odd shape: Sexually perverse
8   Flying loop at top: Quick-thinking
9   Amendments: Neurotic

Capital P

1   2   3   4   5   6

1	Block letter:	Cultured
2	Embellishments:	Vulgar
3	Two parts:	Constructively minded
4	Distorted shape:	Sexually abnormal
5	Loop extended over word:	Generous, protective
6	Claw to left:	Money-minded

Capital Q

1	Simplified:	Clear-thinking
2	Thick horizontal stroke:	(with pressure) Brutal
3	Musical note:	Musical

Capital R

1	Block letter:	Reader
2	Square:	Practical
3	Inflated to loop:	Kind, friendly
4	Loop left:	Egoist
5	Very tall/narrow:	Proud
6	End stroke going down:	Obstinate

Capital S

$ £ S S 5 ƥ
1   2   3   4   5   6

1 Dollar sign: Money-minded, greedy
2 Pound sign: Interested in money
3 Tall: Imaginative
4 Hook to left: Deceitful
5 Angular: Aggressive
6 Start stroke from bottom: Hard worker, difficult

Capital T

T 7 T
1   2 3

1 Over entire word: Patronising
2 Loop to left: Proud
3 Printed: Intelligent

Capital U

U u V
1   2 3

1 Simplified: Unpretentious
2 Wavy line: Versatile
3 Angular: Persistent

Capital V

V V U V
1 2 3 4

1	Simplified:	Clear-minded
2	Second stroke extended:	Enterprising
3	Round:	Unaggressive
4	Looped right:	Disappointed

Capital W

1	Printed:	Cultured
2	Last stroke extended:	Enterprising
3	Round:	Generous
4	Peculiar shape:	Sexually eccentric

Capital X

| 1 | Two parts: | Gossip, muddleheaded |
| 2 | Long end stroke: | Angry |

Capital Y

1	Open to left on underlength:	Impressionable, immature
2	Hook-like stroke:	Avoids responsibility
3	Underlength left:	Homosexual (male)
4	Claw left:	Avaricious
5	Large inflated loop:	Inflated imagination
6	Straight line down:	Good judgment

2 Small Letters

The small letters of the alphabet are mainly in the middle zone: a, c, e, m, n, o, r, s, v, w and x. As the middle zone is the pivot of the writing as a whole small letters have an important part to play in graphological analysis.

Small letters indicate temperament, sociability, or lack of it, honesty or deceit, emotional responses, and whether the writer has a narrow or broad outlook on life. They vary considerably in shape, size and formation, and some small letters have more significance than others. These have been dealt with in more detail – for example the letters f, g, j and y are considered on pp. 109–113 because they reveal factors of the writers' psycho-sexual nature.

Small a

| I | 2 | 3 | 4 | 5 | 6 | 7 | 8 | 9 | 10 | 11 | 12 |

1	Closed:	Discreet, diplomatic
2	Open at top:	Talkative
3	Closed and knotted:	Secretive
4	Narrow:	Narrow-minded
5	Loop to right:	Tactful
6	Loop to left:	Self-deceitful
7	Broad oval:	Imaginative
8	Open at bottom:	Dishonest
9	Filled in:	Jealous
10	Square:	Mechanically-minded

| 11 | Open at left: | Egoistic, greedy |
| 12 | Amendments: | Nervous |

Small b

1	Like figure 6:	Familiar with figures
2	Long starting stroke:	Fussy
3	Without loop:	Intelligent
4	Looped initial stroke:	Proud
5	Looped on end stroke:	Imaginative
6	Printed:	Literary
7	Rounded starting stroke:	Humorous
8	With hook:	Obstinate
9	Enrolled:	Greedy, egoistical
10	Pointed tops:	Resentful
11	Amendments:	Neurotic
12	Initial tick:	Persistent

Small c

1	Narrow:	Shy
2	Angular:	Quick-minded
3	Round:	Gentle
4	Filled in:	Sensual
5	Enrolled:	Shrewd, calculating
6	Stroke underlining whole word:	Self-admiring
7	Concave:	Constructively-minded
8	Block letter:	Reader
9	Stroke extended at top:	Enterprising
10	Small black spot:	Preoccupied with past

11   Square: Mechanically-minded
12   Like small 'e':   Egoistical

Small d

1   Greek: Cultured
2   Curved to right: Pleasure-loving
3   Short stem: Proud
4   Open oval: Talkative
5   Long stem: High ideals and aspirations
6   No loop: Self-confident
7   Sharp at top and bottom: Wilful, resentful
8   Amended: Hypochondriac
9   Stem lower than other   Shrewd
      letters:
10 Musical note: Musical
11 Open at bottom: Hypocritical

Small e

See p. 56

Small f

1   Triangular with back slant: Inhibited emotionally/
                                           sexually
2   Figure 8:   Female homosexual
3   Filled in: Sensual
4   In form of cross: Fatalistic
5   Knotted: Thorough, tough
6   Angular top and bottom: Resentful
7   Block letter: Cultured
8   Large loop at top: Dreamer

9   Narrow and compressed: Repressed emotionally, inhibited
10 Triangular right: Disappointed (sexually)

Small g

See p. 110.

Small h

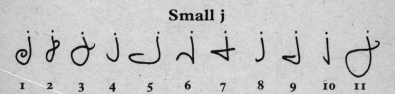

1   High upper loop: Day dreamer, visionary
2   Short upper loop: Unimaginative, realistic
3   Very wide loop: Sensitive, emotional
4   Tall stem: Proud, idealistic
5   Angular top: Resentful
6   Return stroke enrolled: Egoistical
7   Two loops, peculiar shape: Inflated sexual imagination

Small i

See p. 86.

Small j

1   Enrolled: Greedy
2   Figure 8:   Female homosexual
3   Large inflated lower loop: Egoist
4   Loop to left: Sexually irresponsible
5   Horizontally sweeping to left: Male homosexual

6   Claw: Money-minded
7   Triangular loop: Aggressive
8   Open to left: Immature

9 Long loop to left: Impressionable
10 Tick-like stroke: Aggressive
11 Inflated loop (large):   Imaginative

Small k

1 Large loop to right: Rebellious
2 High narrow loop: Religious
3 Knotted: Proud, thorough
4 Stroke going down: Defensive
5 Printed: Literary
6 Underlining stroke: Self-loving
7 Stroke extended at top: Enterprising
8 High and wide loop: Emotional
9 Written as a capital within   Mildly eccentric
      a word:

Small l

1 High and wide: Emotional, sensitive
2 Very high: Visionary
3 No loop: Good judgment
4 Inflated upper loop: Generous
5 Pointed at top: High aspirations
6 Zero form: Interested in money
7 Sharp at bottom: Obstinate

Small m

12	13	14	15	16	

1	Wide and round:	Not always sincere
2	Narrow:	Timid
3	Like w:	Superficial thinker
4	Very rounded top:	Immature, childlike
5	Pointed top:	Critical mind
6	Circle at left:	Jealous
7	Small starting stroke:	Fussy
8	First stroke high:	Egoistic
9	Last stroke high:	Likes to be well thought of
10	High arcades with loops:	Musical
11	Threadlike:	Manipulating
12	Last stroke does not reach base line:	Lacks mental discipline
13	Odd shape:	Sexual quirk
14	Enrolled:	Egoistic, secretive
15	Last stroke flung down:	Temper (if heavy pressure, brutal)
16	Short middle stroke:	Ambitious

Small n

1	2	3	4	5	6	7

1	Last stroke does not reach base line	Ambitious
2	Second stroke high:	Immature
3	Angular top:	Analytically minded
4	Square:	Mechanically minded
5	Broad:	Wasteful
6	Wavy line ending:	Versatile
7	Narrow:	Inhibited

Small o

1	2	3	4	5	6	7

1	Open:	Talkative
2	Closed:	Sometimes talkative but can keep a secret
3	Knotted:	Discreet
4	Zero form:	Money ability
5	Open at base:	Dishonest
6	Large and full:	Emotional, generous
7	Loops within loops:	Insincerity

Small p

1	Stroke extended upwards:	Enterprising
2	Like '&' and 9:	Interested in figures
3	Long lower loop:	Loves physical activity
4	Open at top:	Talkative
5	Printed:	Cultured
6	Two arcs:	Creative

Small q

1	Tick to left:	money-minded
2	Like musical note:	Musical
3	Heavy pressure on downstroke:	Vital, energetic

Small r

1	Larger than other letters:	Eccentric
2	Narrow:	Repressed
3	Looped at top:	Day dreamer

4 End stroke going over: Self-protective
5 Quick 'r':   Quick thinker
6 Like letter 'e':   Artistic
7 Capital instead of small 'r':   Personality quirk

Small s

1 Enrolled: Fussy
2 Closed: Shrewd, secretive
3 Sharp at top: Critical
4 Clawlike: Greedy
5 Angular: Rigid thinker, persistent
6 Tall: Repressed
7 Rounded top: Kind
8 Printed: Reader

Small t

See p. 88.

Small u

1 Wavy line: Versatile
2 Starting stroke: Pull from past
3 Broad and open: Odd imagination

Small v

1 Stroke extended: Enterprising
2 Looped and embellished: Vulgar
3 Simplified: Keen minded, intelligent

4 Rounded: Kindly, non-aggressive

Small w

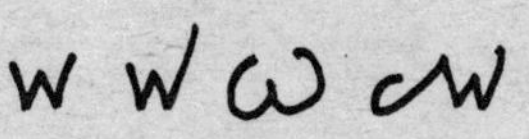

1 2 3 4

1 Angular: Head control
2 End stroke extended: Enterprising
3 Peculiar formation: Has sexual fantasies
4 Hook to left: Resisting

Small x

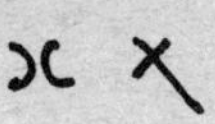

1 2

1 In two parts: Talkative
2 Down stroke extended: Short-tempered

Small y

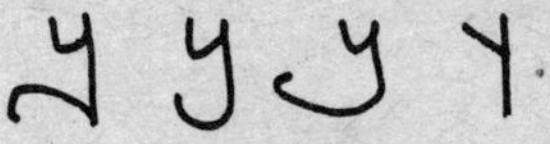

1 2 3 4

1 Claw to left: Greedy
2 Rounded strokes: Kind, friendly
3 Loop to left: Male homosexual
4 Straight line down: Good concentration

Small z

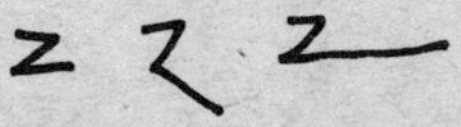

1 2 3

1 Block letter: Reader
2 End stroke going down: Critical
3 End stroke extended: Vain

3 Capital I: The Ego Sign

Capital 'I' is an important letter in graphology. It symbolises the ego, showing how the writer thinks and feels about himself.

The size of the capital 'I' reveals a lot about the writer's personality. If it is made the same size as the rest of the script, it shows the writer has no desire to dominate or put up a façade against the world, but is modestly self-confident, objective and practical.

If it is made much larger than the other capital letters, it shows a lack of inner confidence and an inflated ego. (See Examples 70 and 71.)

I saw the quick

Example 70

magazine,' '9

Example 71

Tiny or small, cramped capital 'I's show timidity; while rounded or enclosed 'I's indicate a desire for self-protection. (See Examples 72 and 73.)

. I completely updated previous year's ed

Example 72

uly so I have
night taming

Example 73

A large ballon-like 'I' is a sign of exaggeration, usually of the writer's own importance, (see Example 74) whereas a simplified plain stroke is a sign of a healthy ego, intelligence and good judgment. (See Example 75.)

I look f
analyses witt

Example 74

I write to tell
mother's favourite

Example 75

Artificial flourishes and loops indicate vulgarity, lack of good taste and a mediocre mind. (See Example 76.) They also express ostentatiousness and a lack of refinement, very often accompanied by limited intellect and excessive vanity.

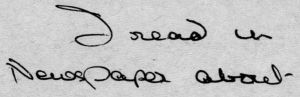

I read in
Newspaper about

Example 76

A printed 'I' shows an interest in literary matters, often literary skill, and reading. (See Example 77.)

Example 77

An 'I' made in the shape of a small 'i' (see Example 78) is a sign of under-valuing the self, and an 'I' written as a figure (7 or 9 or even a 2) can indicate familiarity with figures. (See Examples 79 and 80.) It is also found in the handwriting of people who love

Example 78

Example 79

Example 80

money. The dollar or pound symbols are also reflective of money interest. (These are found in the formation of the small 's' as well.) (See Example 81.)

Example 81

A capital 'I' that leans at a different angle from the rest of the script can be a sign of a guilt complex, particularly if it leans towards the beginning of a word.

An 'I' written in an angular form reveals moderate aggression. (See Example 82.)

Tall, narrow or compressed capital 'I's signify repression or inhibition. (See Example 83.)

Example 82   *Example 83*

4 Small Letter 'i'

It is necessary to take the dots over the 'i' in conjunction with other traits in handwriting because they are slightly less significant than other letter formations, but should not be overlooked. They give away quite a lot about the writer's intention and reaction. The following samples are illustrations of the traits they reveal:

ị	ỉ	˙i	i̇	i̇	i̊	i̓	ī	i̇	i̇	i̇	i̇
1	2	3	4	5	6	7	9	10	11	12	13	14

1 Dot directly above stem: Careful, precise, slightly pedantic, cautious

2 Dot to the right: Enthusiastic, impulsive, quick-thinking, curious

3 Dot to the left: Lacks spontaneity, procrastinates

4 Dot heavy pressure: Materialistic, strong-willed

5 Dot light pressure: Timid, sensitive, easily swayed by stronger personalities

6 Dot in form of circle: Aware of self (often found in young girls' handwriting), egoistical, sense of drama, bid for attention

7 Dot like comma: Witty, sarcastic, sense of humour

8 Different dots: Inconsistent behaviour, imaginative, likes variety

9	Elongated dots:	Touchy under pressure, hasty temper
10	No dot:	Careless, lacks concentration, absent-minded
11	Dot close to stem:	Aggressive, assertive, exacting nature
12	Dot high above stem:	Creative, curious, imaginative
13	Dot in shape of small arc:	Observant
14	Dot club-like:	Brutal, sensual

5 't' Bar Crossing

The letter 't' is one of the most valuable letters of the alphabet to the graphologist and many facets of personality may be deduced from it. The positioning of the bar is of vital importance in showing such factors as leadership and control of others, but it does not suggest lack of confidence when a low bar connects with the following letter. Connecting 't' bar crossings with following or proceeding letters show an outstanding faculty for logical and intellectual combination and usually an ability for research. Such writers may be authors, artists, psychologists, people with intellectual abilities. All the following placings apply to any slant:

1   2   3   4   5   6   7   8   9   10   11   12

13   14   15   16   17   18   19   20   21   22   23   24

25

1   Left of stem, low: Procrastinating, cautious, depressed, feeling of inferiority, lacks essential push and drive

2	Left of stem:	Cautious, moderate
3	High to left:	Inclined to leadership but hesitant to use it
4	Carefully crossed:	Steady, consistent, positive, lacking in forcefulness, has to overcome feelings of inferiority
5	Left/right position:	Able to go forward without dynamic thrust, conscientious
6	Cross starting thin, ending thick:	Slow tempered, (if heavy, pressure, brutal)
7	Cross star shaped:	Sensitive imaginative disappointed
8	Cross slanting up:	Ambitious, curious
9	Cross sloping down:	Depressed, stubborn critical, pessimistic
10	Loop on stem:	Vain, self-approving
11	Two bar cross:	Dual natured
12	Convex:	Self-controlled
13	Sign of cross (religious):	Spiritual background, religious leanings
14	Cross at bottom of stem:	Depressed
15	Hook on end of bar:	Tenacious, fixed opinions
16	Cross starting thick ending thin:	Hasty temper
17	Heavy pressure cross bar:	Determined, quick to anger, firm, strong-willed
18	Light pressure cross bar:	Lacks aggression, easily swayed, sensitive, easily influenced
19	Top of stem bar:	Leadership with caution, tends to daydream
20	Weak cross to right:	Lacks confidence, reluctant to take responsibility
21	Very long 't' bar:	Leadership potential, visionary, imaginative, planning ability, protective

22	Bar right detached	Thoughts running before action, accepts challenge
23	Long, detached, swing towards right:	Highly ambitious, seeks recognition, demanding
24	Very high right:	Intelligent, capacity for executive control, leadership qualities
25	High on top:	Lacks realism, day dreamer

PART FOUR

The Signature

1 The Seal of Self

The signature is the 'Seal of Self'. It reveals how the writer feels about himself and wants the world to see him. The signature has special significance in graphology as an ego symbol.

Very often graphic symbols of a person's profession or work can be seen in his signature. For example, the painter may have a brush, the sailor a ship and the pilot, wings.

The signature also reveals traits of personality and to the trained eye of the graphologist can show the essential characteristics of the writer. However it should not be assessed alone, but only with the rest of the script for an accurate assessment of personality, unless the analyst has considerable experience.

The size, slant and formation of the signature have to be taken into account and judged accordingly. Official and private signatures may differ (possibly different ethics). The surname is representative of the social and collective element; the forename, or initial(s), represents the more private and intimate personality of the writer.

When the signature is identified completely with the script, it shows a natural and unpretentious writer, indicating unchanged behaviour both in business and private life without any façade being presented.

Jimmy Carter (Example 84)

Example 84

Jimmy Carter has a right slanted signature but just a little too much so for someone in a position of great authority. It shows a lack of emotional control under tension or stress. The tall upper loops to his name show his spiritual interests and aspirations, while the threadlike strokes in the middle of 'Jimmy' are seen in the handwriting of many politicians, betraying manipulating powers, sometimes with doubtful purpose.

The whole signature reveals an emotional man, who under pressure would be subjective in his judgment rather than objective.

Richard Nixon (Example 85)

Nixon reveals in his signature – taken at three different periods in his life – how his mental and physical deterioration can be seen with amazing clarity.

He starts off with a reasonably clear and legible signature with a sociable right slant to it. His next signature shows snake-like strokes coming out demonstrating how he has learned to manipulate and practise deceit. His third signature shows he is mentally racing against time, the signature becoming less and less clear or legible in the process. The fourth signature, without a shred of legible script, shows that manipulation has given way to lying, deceitfulness and dishonesty. The pressure is also weaker, indicating his physical strength at a low ebb.

Gerald Ford (Example 86)

There is a lack of intellectual depth and self-dependence in this signature. Ford, with these rather long vulgar and embellished letters, has an exaggerated desire to impress. There is a longing for real or imagined greatness shown in the way he forms his capital 'G', and the lower clawlike stroke at the bottom of his capital 'F' shows that he is money-conscious and enjoys material success. There is no compromise in this writing. Ford would take drastic action to solve a problem rather than use logic and reason. The loops of his small 'd's demonstrate personal vanity, although the legibility of the signature shows his honesty and conscientiousness.

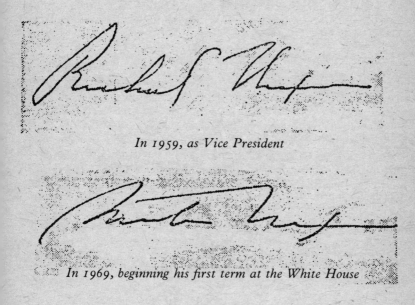

Richard Nixon's changing signature

In 1959, as Vice President

In 1969, beginning his first term at the White House

Shortly before his resignation
Example 85

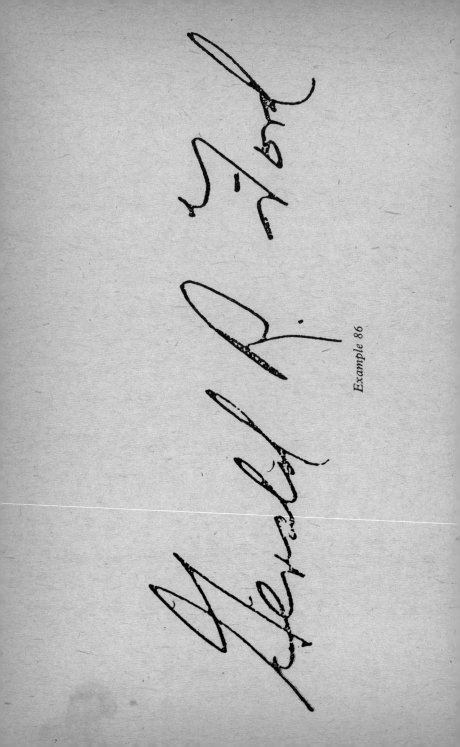

Example 86

Mary (Example 87)

Example 87   Mary

Mary has an angular signature which shows her to possess moderate aggression in her make up. The strokes are lean without any warmth or affection in them (no loops) and the left slant shows her introverted and introspective nature. The spiky tops to her 'm's and 'n's indicate a degree of sarcasm and sharpness of tongue. The elongated 'i' dot is a sign of irritability under pressure and sensitivity bordering on the neurotic.

Eric (Example 88)

Thursday.

Yours sincerely,

Example 88   Eric

Eric lacks confidence in himself and his timid signature expresses his mild inferiority complex. It is small, almost apologetic, showing he lacks drive. Yet the rising lines indicate optimism and even ambition. The heavy pressure and the thick 'i' dot are signs of materialism. He places a period after his name, confirming his caution and general mistrust.

Jennifer (Example 89)

Example 89   Jennifer

Jennifer does not show much consistency in her writing, her script lacks rhythm and this is reflected in the varying slants. Her signature has more pressure in the first name, showing a desire to attract attention to herself, and the threadlike lines in her surname are a sign that she is able to manipulate. (This signature has been reduced to half actual size.)

Jerry (Example 90)

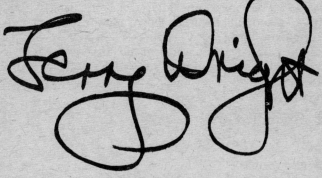

Example 90   Jerry

The flourished and vulgar upper and lower loops to this signature are exaggerated, pointing to a vain and egoistical personality. They display a liking for admiration and attention, and an over-active imagination with sexual overtones.

Allan (Example 91)

Example 91   Allan

Allan has a suicide signature because he not only encircles his name, but cancels himself out by stroking a line through his signature as well. The left slant shows his withdrawal, and the drooping lines of his writing reveal his depression. The inflated upper and lower loops indicate his mental conflict and the heavy pressure is a sign of anger.

Writing pressure is often increased because of the innate energy it produces. Happiness or joy has the opposite effect and often results in a light pressured script.

Peter (Example 92)

Example 92   Peter

Peter has threadlike writing and this is carried over into his signature. He can be diplomatic, tactful and uses his psychological talent for dealing with people. There is insight and manipulating ability shown in this signature. Because his signature is the same size as his script, he does not put up any façade, but the wavy stroke in the middle of his words is a sign of the opportunist and Peter's undoubted adaptability enables him to run with the hare and hunt with the hounds.

Paul (Example 93)

Religious mania is shown in the odd looking signature of Paul, who has lost his sense of reality. The huge inflated loop covering his name shows his muddleheadedness. He has also drawn a line through his signature and the large script denotes his feelings of superiority springing from an inferiority complex and his mental instability.

Example 93   Paul

Paul (Example 94)

Paul is an actor and his signature reveals his somewhat flamboyant personality and need to express it. The large writing is a sign of his egoism, while the speed of his script indicates his quickness of mind and fluency.

Example 94   Paul

Margaret (Example 95)

The slightly rising slope to Margaret's signature shows that she has a basically optimistic nature; the roundness of her letters indicates warmth, and the large spaces between her capital letters and the next letter reveal her well developed intuition. The downstrokes to her small 'g' show her concentration and sense of fatalism.

Margaret Scott

Example 95   Margaret

John (Example 96)

By circling his signature, John shows an introverted nature that seeks to protect itself. This is also confirmed by his left slant. The whole signature is cramped and narrow, showing that he shies away from reality imposed by the outside world and people.

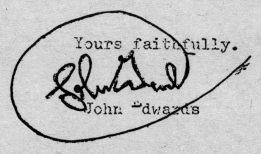

Example 96   John

Diana (Example 97)

Diana is a writer and her creativity almost 'leaps' from the page for the pen hardly seems to touch the paper. Her signature is like an abstract drawing and the thread-like stroke at the end, tapering off into a line, shows her considerable manipulating powers. (This signature has been reduced to half its actual size.)

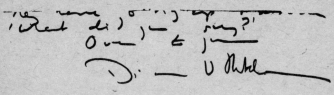

Example 97   Diana

2   The Choice of Colour

The colour of the ink is of significance, though not of paramount importance. Blue-black is the universal colour, certainly in business. It indicates that the user is reasonably conventional, and has no leanings to exhibitionism or to be regarded as out of the ordinary.

Here are indications of what ink colours show:

Blues: In general, blue goes with outward going natures, and is associated with warmth, sincerity, understanding, loyalty, inspiration and often with the more spiritually minded.

Royal blue: If purposely chosen, as it often is by nurses, welfare officers and those engaged in service to others, it indicates a warm, well-disposed nature, equable in disposition and sympathy.

Turquoise blue: This is often preferred by women but is used by men too. It is linked with the artistic temperament and shows enthusiasm and a desire to be noticed.

Washy blue: Banal and unimaginative.

Black: This is often used by leaders and executive types. It is a bold, assertive colour, and those who prefer it are ambitious. Women who choose it are generally career-minded.

Dark brown: Users of this like to be noticed. They are often people in authority, such as doctors, draughtsmen and people with a sense of responsibility.

Watery pale ink: This is preferred by those with an artistic temperament, such as writers, musicians, poets, and often indicates a vein of seriousness which can lead to depression.

Red: This is popular with people who want to feel 'different', and indeed often are, such as schoolmasters, lawyers, lecturers and people in professional positions, though red ink is often used deliberately to make the writing stand out – for example, in making corrections and amendments. When used as a personal choice it shows ambition, generosity and energy but, according to the script, these can come from a pompous know-all.

Green: This is favoured by individualists and those who do not want to be one of a crowd. They often have links in the artistic field, and are adaptable, versatile, mentally alert and of good intelligence. It is often favoured by younger people. If the form level is low, it indicates an inferiority complex.

Violet: This, especially if used on tinted or coloured paper, points to fussiness and a desire on the part of the writer to show off.

3   Envelope Addresses

The placing of the address on an envelope, together with the slant of the writing, can show a great deal. Sometimes the outward appearance is seen in the address but the letter will provide the inner disposition.

If the address is placed in the centre, it shows clear thinking, organising ability, balance, orderliness, care and consideration.

If the address is placed:

Too high: It signifies hastiness, carelessness, and someone who is not unduly influenced by material consideration and is a dreamer.

Too low: It denotes pessimism.

To the right: It shows a person inclined to seek advice and help, who has little inclination to take initiative, is outward looking but is restless and emotional.

Top left: Indicates a reserved reflective writer who prefers to rely on self, is not obliging, egocentric, shy, possibly forbidding and afraid of the future.

Top right: The writer is uninhibited and seeks freedom of expression without fear of consequences. He can be a strong idealist with perfectionist tendencies. In young people it indicates conflict with rules and authority.

Bottom left: It indicates strong materialistic influences, suspicion, caution, envy and doubt about other people.

Bottom right: Shows a desire for freedom based on a strong materialistic streak. Such writers seek to escape from past environmental experiences. They have no illusions and require that everything must be on a firm base.

The address extends from the top left to the bottom right: This shows caution, suspicion and a hesitant approach to strangers.

The address is illegible: Signifies psychological difficulty in observing conventional considerations and communications, difficulty in adapting, trouble in social intercourse and lack of harmony.

Stylised or embellished: The demeanour of the writer masks his real personality.

Name and address underlined: The writer cannot distinguish degrees of importance, emphasises trifles and demands appreciation of trivialities.

Comparison with script inside

If the writing on the envelope is identical with that of the letter inside it shows the writer to be natural, frank and unpretentious.

If completely different, it shows the writer hides his or her real feelings, and outward behaviour does not always reflect the writer's real feelings.

If the writing on the envelope is more right slanted than the text of the letter, the writer is putting up a show of warmth or goodwill which may lack sincerity.

PART FIVE

Symbolism in Graphology

1 Sexual Symbols of 'g' and 'y'

The lower loops or strokes of the small letters 'g' and 'y' give clues to the writer's sexual preferences and instinctive drives, and also his emotional attitudes generally. It is here that tensions, strengths or weaknesses are seen, and whether the writer is active or passive sexually. Impotence in men and frigidity in women can be seen in the downstrokes of 'g' and 'y', if they are weak, neglected and fail to cross over the loop, unless there is illness or physical disability.

Sexual inadequacy can be seen and the reason for it traced to the mental, emotional or physical, caused through illness, or even guilt.

Inflated loops show the writer who has an exaggerated sexual imagination and is preoccupied with the erotic or sensual.

Gentle, even loops and rounded writing reveal the writer who has no sexual fixations and who has a balanced attitude to the instinctive drives.

Long, even loops pushed to the left are frequently found in the script of homosexuals or men with a strong mother fixation – the Freudian 'Oedipus complex'.

Open underlengths that do not cross over but are wide and open, show the dreamer, the gullible and the immature. They also indicate the romantic.

A 'g' or 'y' in the form of a figure 8 is often found in the handwriting of female homosexuals. It can also be a sign of literary talent. (See Example 98A.)

Example 98A   Three samples of female homosexual script

The triangular loop is a sign of sexual disappointment, and is found in the writing of domestic tyrants and people who are resentful of their partner. When seen in female handwriting, it reveals the bossy woman or dominant female disappointed through frustration. When seen in male writing, it reveals the man who is unhappy, resentful and who feels trapped or inhibited, perhaps because he is with the wrong partner.

Any left swing to the underlengths of 'g' and 'y' indicates links that bind the writer to past emotional and environmental experiences and influence, and a writer who has difficulty in breaking these ties. When seen in male writing, it usually signifies an Oedipus complex (i.e. a mother fixation). (See Example 98B.)

Very long, sharp and narrow underlengths that dip into the upper or middle zone of the next line indicate a pre-occupation with the instinctive drives and inability to cope with them, causing conflict.

Clawlike loops to the left are a sign of avarice.

Lower loops or strokes to the right, signify the future, and also that the writer's father's influence prevails.

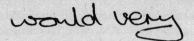

Example 98B   Left swing loop in male homosexual script

Underlengths small 'g' and 'y'

ϱ	ʯ	ɡ	ʯ	ϙ	ϙ	ʯ	ϙ
1	2	3	4	5	6	7	8

ϙ	ʯ	ϐ	ʯ	ϙ	ʯ	ϙ	8
9	**10**	**11**	**12**	**13**	**14**	**15**	**16**

1	Straight line down:	Concentrated, fatalistic, good judgment
2	Normal loop:	Warm, imaginative, demonstrative
3	Triangular loop:	Domestically tyrannical, emotionally or sexually disappointed

4	Open to left:	Emotionally immature, impressionable (often found in young girls' script)
5	Tick to right:	Mildly aggressive
6	Tick to left:	Aggressive
7	Large inflated loops:	Inflated sexual imagination
8	Clawstroke left:	Avoids responsibility (often sexual), avarice
9	Long downstroke (with pressure)	Materialistic, physically energetic
10	Neglected underlengths:	Physically weak, little need for or interest in sex (may be illness)
11	Enrolled:	Greedy
12	Stroke upwards right:	Altruistic
13	Underlength cut off at bottom:	Sexually anxious
14	Island at bottom:	Needs security
15	Turned inwards no crossing:	Sexually inhibited, repressed of instinctive drives
16	Like figure eight:	Female homosexual – can also be literary sign

Triangular underlengths (Example 99)

Example 99A   *Example 99B   The 'domestic tyrant'*

When the underlengths are triangular one sees the domestic tyrant: the type who must be boss in the home. This particular handwriting where the 'g' and 'y' forms a triangle is a sign of disappointment in the choice of sexual partner and sometimes shows itself in the writing of women who either want to be the dominant partner or who have had this role thrust upon them.

There is aggression and resentment in this writer and even in sexual activity a dominance of personality. Such writers often become a little overbearing but have a strong protective streak.

Left underlength (Example 100)

Example 100A   Example 100B   *Underlength with left swing*

The left swing of the underlengths in this writing indicates the writer's mother fixation. These left swings are usually found in the handwriting of male homosexuals and show the links that bind him to the past and his parental conflicts.

There is usually a strong affection – or hatred – for the mother; frequently many homosexual men express a lot of self love in their attitudes. This writer has a fertile erotic imagination and this shows in the large inflated loops.

Open loops going to the left

Example 101A   Example 101B   *Poetic attitude to sex*

The writer, whose loops going left are open, has an almost poetic attitude towards sex. She is open to sensual impressions, has a tendency to daydream and doesn't really want to come down to earth. There is a need to cling to illusions and live in a fairy tale world where the emotions are concerned. The writer is looking for a knight in shining armour to carry her off. (See Example 101.)

Passionate underlengths (Example 102)

Example 102A   Example 102B   *Strong sex drive*

Long heavy looped underlengths show that the writer has an extremely strong sexual drive and is interested in materialistic things. The writer is basically down-to-earth and has not a lot of time to spare for pie in the sky or fairies at the bottom of the garden.

He is interested in the physical side of life rather than the spiritual, and is able to cope with the sexual demands of his nature, having a strong constitution and considerable energy. The pressure of the writing shows this, and a passionate and demanding nature too.

2 Punctuation Marks, Dots and Commas

Excessive punctuation marks – too many dots or commas – express a desire to show off, fussiness, a tendency to exaggerate or over-emphasise the writer's viewpoint, or one who will make trifles sound more important than they really are. It also indicates sentimentality.

The omission of full stops and other punctuation marks, together with low form level, points to illiteracy. The writer should not be dismissed as being obtuse and self-centred, although the writing points in that direction.

3   Doodling

A doodle is a design or picture scribbled while one is thinking about something else. Yet like any other form of graphic expression it reveals many traits of personality. Most doodles are written unconsciously and therefore give a good indication of hidden desires, hopes, fears, anxieties or ambitions. There are many types of doodle and each supplies a clue to the emotional side of the scribbler, often revealing unsuspected facets of his personality. Doodles are, in fact, diagrams of the unconscious.

Psychologists regard doodles as projections of repressed emotions and thoughts, and they are often used in assessing personality in psycho-analysis.

Even the would-be amateur psychologist can, with a little know-how, interpret the meaning behind these 'nonsense pictures', as they are sometimes called.

Relatives, friends, boss, the executive at the conference table, the typist at her shorthand pad, the PA at the telephone, all betray facets of their personalities and unconscious wishes when they have a pen in hand and start doodling.

Doodles can reveal symptoms, and give a message from the unconscious that something is wrong. They can be a warning of a disturbed emotional state, or a secret fear, and provide clues to the writer's inner conflicts.

Doodles can be classified amongst others as social, sexual, sadistic, angry, romantic, obsessional, creative or neurotic, according to their many shapes, sizes and forms. Here are the most common examples.

Squares or boxes

Squares or boxes all reveal a feeling of being trapped or caught up in, perhaps, an emotional life that is causing claustrophobic feelings.

Faces

Faces come into two categories – happy and grotesque. Groups of faces are a sign of gregariousness and a desire for a social life, for mixing and meeting with all types. A face on its own, if jovial, indicates again, sociability, a need for companionship and love; if grotesque, morose or distorted it reveals dissatisfaction and resentment.

Mazes, webs, puzzles

Again, these are indications of the doodler who is frustrated, baffled, in a dilemma, or has some inner conflict.

Large doodles

Complicated, large expansive and often coloured doodles are usually evidence of the artistic and creative and also of initiative.

Shaded strokes

Filled in doodles, with heavy pressure or shaded strokes show tension, anxiety and secret worry sometimes amounting to fear.

Circles and flowing lines

Flowers, hearts, round circles (the ring without end), curved or flowing lines, animals, plants and leaves, all reveal a basically affectionate, kind and loving nature.

Sharp angular tips

Sharp pointed strokes, guns, spiky angles, arrows with sharp tips, weapons of all sorts, ropes and whips all demonstrate a violent and aggressive nature and even hostility or anti-social behaviour.

Oddly shaped letters

Oddly shaped letters, usually a 'B' or a 'W', faces, lips, shoes (fetishes) candles, church spires, phallic symbols, sexual organs, reveal a preoccupation with the erotic and lower instinctive urges.

Ropes, arrows

Hanging ropes, whip-like strokes, gallows or arrows which often appear in the signature, indicate varying degrees of sadistic tendencies.

Bare trees

Bleak and bare trees, narrow faces, thin figures, weary drooping lines, narrow houses without doors or window, all reveal a lack of warmth, and repression or inhibition of the emotions.

Flowers

Hearts, initials entwined, pretty flowers and plants, little houses with curtained windows, smoke coming out of the chimney, and a garden, or flourishing trees in leaf or bearing fruit, all signify a compassionate, affectionate and warmhearted nature.

Travel symbols

Doodles in the shape of ships, planes, boats or cars are an indication of the doodler who wants to 'get away from it all'. They are often by male doodlers and the heavier the pressure, the more the writer wants to escape.

Three dimensional

This type of doodle expresses keenness of mind, constructive planning ability, intellectual capacity, fluency of thought.

Animals

Very often drawn by young girls, these show the dreamer and the non-aggressive personality; if the animals are curled, it sometimes indicates a need for security.

Numbers

These are significant if they are doodled over and over again, showing perhaps pre-occupation with figures or money.

Repeated doodles

A design or formation that is constantly doodled over and over again and again, is a sign of an obsession. Very often the figure 8 appears in such doodles.

Example 103: Imaginative, versatile, and because of the shading in and slight filling up of the doodles, a lively and extremely active mind.

Example 103

Example 104: Cats and flowers: This is a non-aggressive personality but the mildly angular strokes indicate sensitivity and mild touchiness.

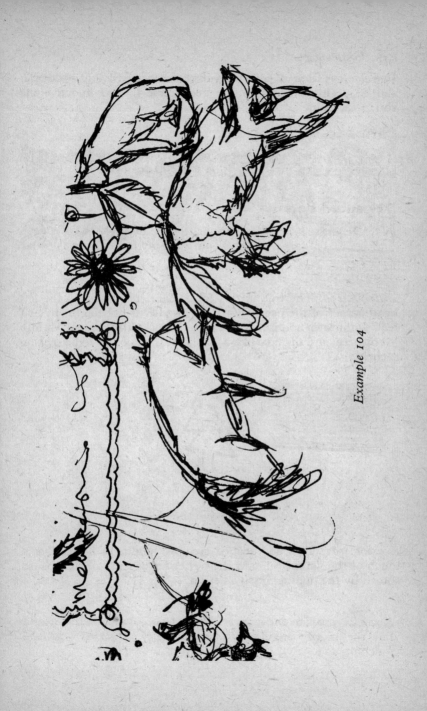

Example 104

Example 105: Lots of faces, revealing the sociability of the doodler and his desire to be with other people and to lead an active and varied social life.

Example 105

Example 106: The tree in this form, bare and drawn in the left hand corner of the page, shows the doodler is not too happy and feels withdrawn and isolated. There is a lack of emotional warmth in this tree, and the box-like base shows the doodler to be seeking security.

Example 106

Example 107: This odd shaped creature holding a flower, has a touch of the whimsical, and the writer has a sense of the absurd shown by the non-aggressive design.

Example 107

Example 108: Again a flower, but this time one that has a certain amount of sexuality in its formation, and the shading round the edges could be a slight feeling of apprehension on the part of the doodler about her sexuality.

Hon Sec.

Example 108

Example 109: Muddle or design? This doodle shows an active and imaginative person, but the maze and the squares are a sign of frustration with a likelihood of impetuous action.

Example 109

Example 110: These boxes are carefully and thoughtfully drawn. They imply a feeling of being trapped, but the doodler does not fill them in, which indicates that he has the confidence to solve his problems – by thinking, rather than rushing into action.

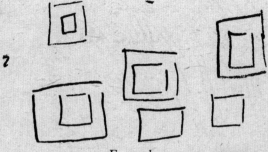

Example 110

Example 111: Hearts, flowers, houses with smoke – a symbolic doodle typical of many young people, showing the complete romantic and the desire for emotional fulfilment.

Example 111

4 Numerals

Numbers relate to material things and values. The way they are written can be revealing.

Smoothly written numbers: Indicate the writer with a practical attitude towards material values, who is methodical and business-like.

Small, sharp and concise figures: Show regular involvement and concentration on monetary or financial matters, typical of account-ants, mathematicians, executives or physicists.

Indistinct (allowing different interpretations): A negligently in-different or neurotic attitude to material values, sometimes a blurring of monetary issues in favour of the writer.

Touched up figures: Show uncertainty or anxiety over financial matters, especially if the rest of the script is clear.

Decorative or embellished figures: Indicate the daydreamer with indifference to money for its own sake.

Very large figures: Show a materialistic but impractical nature.

Clumsy, heavy pressure with figures: Shows materialism but no money sense.

Neat well-formed, legible figures: Indicate reliability and honesty.

PART SIX

Graphology at Work

1 Building up an Analysis

Before building up a full analysis, the professional graphologist has six requirements, though it is not always possible to meet them. They are:

1 A sample, the longer the better, that has not been written specifically for analysis.
2 Writing on unlined paper where there is no guidance to affect the slant or variation of spacing natural to the writer.
3 Preferably a full signature rather than the surname and initials of the forename(s).
4 The reason for the analysis. Whether it is for vocational guidance, personnel selection, character and personality assessment, for advice on marriage compatability or intelligent self-interest by the writer.
5 The writer's sex.
6 The writer's age.

Age and sex are the two things which handwriting does not reveal with any certainty, although it is possible after long experience to assess both.

The student who has grasped the basic concepts and is graduating to the stage when he can build up an analysis may sensibly concentrate first on the handwriting of people he knows. Start off by examining carefully:

1 *The zones*, and any departure from normal.
2 *The slant*, left, upright or to the right.
3 *Connecting strokes*, and the variety, i.e. angular, garland, arcade or thread.

4 *The form level* as a whole, including margins, spacing and regularity.
5 *The base line*, wavy or not.
6 *The pressure*, whether heavy, light, medium or pasty.
7 *Size* of script, large, medium or small.
8 *Speed*, slow, fast or average.

Make a note of them and their interpretation, and once these basic traits have been established, it will be possible with the added help of the graphologist's ABC to build up a sound analysis.

Very soon the student will build up his own collection of different forms of handwriting and his own ABC. But it cannot be stressed too often that over-emphasis of one or two single features can be misleading. As many as possible of the other traits must be taken into consideration before coming to a firm conclusion.

Intuition and psychological insight can and do play a part in graphology, but scientific graphology relies on the patterns and lines presented on a sheet of paper which are the language and imagery of the mind and heart of the writer. Interpretation should be kept to the traits shown in the graphic material sent for analysis, objectively and without preconceived concepts from any other source.

The student who has progressed to this point and has opened the door to a new world of understanding of his fellow men will appreciate that others have gone deeper. Some of the thoughts of Jung will be of practical value.

2   The Four Psychic Functions

Analytical psychology divides people into two categories, the extrovert and the introvert. Jung went further and separated people into four functional types:

> Thinking
> Feeling
> Sensation
> Intuition

The four functions are not usually developed equally in one person. One or the other is generally predominant.

Jung calls Thinking and Feeling rational functions, such as love and hate, truth or falsehood. He calls Sensation and Intuition irrational functions because they deal with perceptions and cannot be evaluated. Thus:

Thinking responds to the environment or a particular situation by way of logic;

Feeling sees things as good or bad, it accepts or rejects according to outlook and experience;

Sensation is the reaction to things as they appear to be without forming any sort of judgment;

Intuition is the ability to see with inner perception beneath the surface and react quickly without any apparent reason or thought.

Handwriting shows the relative strength of these functions or which dominates as:

Thinking: This is shown by small simplified writing, good spacing between lines and words, with the upper zone possibly emphasised and the use of original forms. Very often the lower zone letters 'g' and 'y' will have a single downstroke without a loop.

Feeling: This is shown by over-large letters, full letters, garland script and right slant.

Sensation: This is shown by pasty or smeary writing, right slant, inflated upper and lower loops and particularly exaggerated lower loops.

Intuition: This is shown by light pressure, disconnected writing, and capitals that stand apart from the rest of the script.

It will be easy to define which of the four functions is dominant in a script where the psychological type of writer is pronounced. It is more difficult to classify where the personality is not so pronounced. For instance, by studying the four graphic indications above, it will be seen that pasty, smeary or smudged writing will indicate the type of personality who will over-indulge the senses by eating, drinking, and with sex. The person who is highly sensitive and easily hurt will have light pressure and rhythmic writing.

Bearing this in mind, the student making a reasonably full analysis should look for the following traits:

Positive	*Negative*
Adaptable	Critical
Ambitious	Nervous
Altruistic	Suspicious
Emotionally controlled	Insincere
Firm	Inert
Kind	Cold
Sociable	Aggressive
Self-disciplined	Weak (of will)
Original	Immature
Imaginative	Withdrawn
Mature	Superficial

3 The Introvert and Extrovert

The introvert

The signs of introversion are the left slant, which is possibly the main trait, and left tendencies in the script as a whole in all three zones. Apart from slant, the formation of 'w' and 'd' indicate introversion because the end stroke turns inwards or backwards instead of finishing on the endstroke down. If this stroke is seen in children's handwriting, the tendency can be corrected.

The introvert cannot adapt easily to the outside world because he is introspective and this will be reflected in handwriting that leans away from the normal right slant but towards the left, revealing an emotionally sensitive nature, critical sense, inhibitions and repression.

The traits associated with introversion are:

Positive	*Negative*
Analytically minded	Self-conscious
Imaginative	Tends to self-analyse
Attentive to detail	Shy
Methodical in approach	Reserved
Reflective	Lacks confidence
Sensitive	Inhibited
Creative (often artistic talent)	Repressed emotionally
	Anxious

The extrovert

The signs of extroversion are a right slant, rounded and medium large writing, long ending strokes and small even spaces between words. The extrovert, because of his social nature, will direct his energies outwards and towards future goals. He goes all out to meet people and is emotionally more responsive and receptive than the introvert.

His reactions are more spontaneous and he has the self-confidence and adjustability to make successful friendships and relationships.

The traits associated with extroversion are:

Positive	*Negative*
Self-confident	Careless
Friendly	Impatient
Sociable	Lacks attention to detail
Warm	Hasty in making decisions
Enthusiastic	Impulsive
Persuasive	Lacks planning ability
Sales ability	Reckless
Active	

4 Children's Handwriting

It is often stated that it is the school teacher who makes us write the way we do. This of course is just not so. Every child develops his own style of writing. Some children stick to the copybook form all their lives, but with the majority, their handwriting develops as their personality expands and they form a distinctive style.

With the advancement of age, the pattern becomes more and more clear and the child emerges into a personality in his own right, his handwriting becomes exclusively his. Many young people are ready to have their handwriting analysed at an early age. Even so, this can present problems as some children are mature at eleven, some are still very immature in their late teens, and many have difficulty in forming letters and words even at a much later age. Many schools teach the same method of writing, but there are different styles of penmanship taught in this country today. This means that if a child has been sent to two or three different schools in various parts of the country, his writing may show three apparently conflicting forms of lettering.

Problems in children show up clearly in their handwriting. For example, many inhibitions and conflicts are expressed through cramped or overcrowded script, or in a left hand slant, which can point to anti-social behaviour and depression, as well as a state of anxiety.

Aggression

Signs of aggression or tension (two signs of delinquent behaviour) will come across in a child's handwriting – angular strokes, spikey script and angular writing. A script that is flowing freely and is of a medium size with good formations and rounded strokes, indicates the child who is well-balanced and shows emotional stability to cope with the minor crisis that crops up, and his writing will be free of conflict.

Overstroking (Example 112)

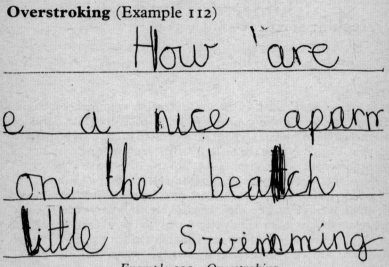

Example 112   Overstroking

Going over letters more than once or twice is a neurotic sign, and in children's handwriting shows that something is not quite as it should be in the personality structure. The problem is causing the child apprehension and nervous anxiety.

Artistic (Example 113)

Example 113   Artistic

This large script reveals a need for the child to express his personality, and he should be encouraged to develop any artistic or creative talents he may have. The upright script also shows emotional repression and his inability to 'let go' his emotions.

Irregular script (Example 114)

Must go to bed now. See you soon (u ron)

love Nik.

Don't work too hard; it's only money you get.

Example 114   Irregular script

Nicky has a very irregular script, indicating that his concentration could be better than it is. He is easily distracted. The downward slope of his writing shows that he is not on top of the world at the time of writing – this may be a momentary thing; the erratic rhythm of his script shows his need for variation and change; the pressure reveals energy and drive.

Obsessional writing (Example 115)

Vous aimez le cinéma?
Vous aimez la radio?
Vous aimez les animaux?

Example 115   Obsessional script

This writer is a young girl who has carried legibility to extremes. She has given up any individuality in her writing. The carefully formed letters and words shows that she is under a lot of tension, and the slight left slant of her monotonous script indicates that emotionally she is incapable of change and variety. The rounded strokes are signs of a basically non-aggressive personality with a lack of push and drive. The pressure shows the tension she is experiencing.

Filling in (Example 116)

f inis hed ne put the pain

on the floor at the Back

Example 116   Filling in

If a child persists in filling in many of his letters, (usually the small 'o' and 'a') and uses heavy pressure to do so, he may have a slight fear or anxiety that is worrying him. Perhaps he is unhappy at home or school; any shading-in or filling in, should be watched, and the apprehension brought out in the open so that it can be dealt with.

Autistic (Example 117)

What Is youi

My name is I

How old are

Example 117   Autistic

This abnormally large writing belongs to a child who is autistic but slowly improving. The margin on the left is getting wider, a sign indicating a feeling of insecurity and being 'got at', while the straight capital 'I' shows he could pick things up quickly and he is able to distinguish space well. His writing improves both in size and spacing towards the bottom of the letter showing that his concentration is also increasing.

Abnormally large script (Example 118)

next week End We
go nome you woul
much like To See !

Example 118   Abnormally large script

This writing shows a sign of a physically active (over-active at times) child, lacking in concentration, who loves admiration and attention. She is materialistic and likes doing everything on a grand scale. There are also signs of an obsession with the home and family (middle zone). The other two zones – the upper and lower – are neglected in her script, and she has channelled her energies into the middle zone – the day to day sphere of her life.

Sam (12 years) (Example 119)

ie box.   We   Empty   Our

eave   the   Water   Jar

board.   we   leave   the

Example 119   Sam

This sample of handwriting with its long rolled up underlengths indicates a preoccupation with the physical. Sam needs to take part in as many exercises as possible, sports, walking, running, and so on, to use up that considerable energy and vitality.

The left slant reveals self-consciousness while the open legible writing demonstrates his need to show off – it is a bid for attention. The downward slope reveals mild depression, and the use of capitals where small letters should be, demonstrates mild eccentricity, even at his early age.

Charlotte (Example 120)

Charlotte is eight and her writing shows her ability to form individual letters in her own style. Her 't' bar crossings are slightly wavy, and her spacing is wide and clear, showing her ability for intelligent thinking. The 'i' dots are carefully placed above the stem showing a good eye for detail, and the high arcade of her small 'm's show that she could develop an ear for music. There are no signs of instability in this writing.

Juliet (Example 121)

Juliet (her twin sister) shows a little more maturity in her writing, and the way she forms her letters. The bold round script indicates confidence and intelligence, the slightly rising and downward trend to the lines reveal that she is perhaps more moody than Charlotte. The writing is free from tension, and is harmonious and well balanced.

black moods of
intment Rachel
y fossil now a
ballerina
          Charlotte

Example 120   Charlotte

paper   bags and
   peel and lemonade

about and she

very upset at the

          Juliet.

Example 121   Juliet

5 Alcoholism

There are an estimated over 800,000 alcoholics in this country and they come from all classes of society. Besides causing a lot of misery to other people, they do a lot of harm to themselves, mentally and physically. Some end up in mental hospitals, while others, if they are fortunate, come under the wing of Alcoholics Anonymous, and are helped back to a normal life.

Research into the handwriting of alcoholics has shown that the degree of inebriety can be seen with clarity. (See Example 122.) Graphology can detect the common traits in the writing of alcoholics who possess many conflicts apart from the problem of drink. An examination of handwriting will show the emotional and mental disposition of the writer and the motives that led to his introduction to his over-indulged drinking habits.

Many alcoholics attempt to escape other problems and difficulties by resorting to drink. Their drinking is perhaps only a symptom of a very disturbed personality. Features that stand out in the writing of most of these people are lack of self-control, irritability and unreliability. At the present time, more and more young people are rapidly becoming alcoholics. The latest report issued by the Home Office shows a sharp rise in teenage drinking habits over the past few years.

Many causes can be named when trying to pinpoint the reason for anyone becoming addicted to alcohol. Among these are matrimonial troubles, frustration in work or career, at home and in the emotional sphere.

Handwriting analysis can assist in diagnosing the extent of the problem, and the motive behind it. Most handwriting of inebriates shows fraying and jerky strokes, trembling lines, and the writing may appear as smeary with shaky up-and-down strokes, due to defective muscular control. There may be interruptions in the rhythm of the script and heavy uneven lines indicating depression and general unhappiness.

There is also a lack of co-ordination evident in their handwriting, which is manifested in the movement of the script; sometimes this is slow and ponderous. The use of corrections and deletions mar the writing too, particularly the constant use of the dot over the letter 'i' which all indicate that the writer lacks concentration. Broken strokes and lines of handwriting slanting downwards are also signs of inebriety.

When the lower parts of the letters 'g' and 'y' are neglected, this reveals physical weakness, as well as mental inability to cope with sexual problems.

Very often a page of handwriting will suggest a row of illegible scribbling, and frequently shows a left slant, indicating a desire to withdraw from society and the usual social contacts.

Example 122   Alcoholic script

6 Dishonesty

Dishonesty comes in many forms; it can be emotional, mental or downright criminal. The motivations are many and varied. Why do people become dishonest? In their handwriting there are unmistakable signs of motivation that can be seen.

Fear, worry and guilt are often feelings that lead to dishonesty, so if we look at a person's handwriting, and find one or several of these traits combined with established traits that denote deceit, we know we have an individual who may not be trusted.

A script that cannot keep to a straight base line, and has small 'a's and 'o's open at the base, is a cardinal sign of dishonesty in graphology. If the 't' bar is weak, it shows the personality who is easily led and lacks willpower. If the letters are overstroked (touched up or with several strokes to the same letter) this is a sign of a neurotic personality, possibly suffering from anxiety, and if the pressure accompanying these strokes is uneven throughout, a degree of unreliability is indicated.

Exaggerated or artificial capitals with enrollments and embellishments, mean the writer has an exaggerated ego and enjoys being well thought of; he thinks he is more important than he is, and may lie to achieve his aims, claiming credit for things to which he is not entitled, and so on.

7　Opportunism

Letters and words that have threadlike strokes are the sign of psychological talent and manipulating power. The writer is able to get his own way by flattery, persuasion and using people to his advantage. Thread writing is nearly always found in the handwriting of opportunists, or quick-witted people.

Small letters that vary in size are another sign to look for, because, if the height is variable and uneven, the person may be undergoing some sort of mental conflict, preventing him from being open and straightforward.

Letters and figures that are constantly split into two parts and small letters omitted in words can also demonstrate that the writer may not be completely honest.

8   Forgery

Fluent or rapid motion is almost impossible in cases of forgery or forged documents, the tempo is inevitably slow and the writing very often laboured with many stops for concentration; although interrupted strokes are possibly only seen under a microscope. Further many forgers when not satisfied with their work, re-touch it, and this results in the re-touching being done at varying angles of the pen.

Anonymous letters

With anonymous letters there are certain traits that the writer overlooks, such as margins, spaces between letters and words, the size and rhythm of the script, and invariably the writer will start the letter at the same spot on the page on which he normally begins his own everyday letters. Retraced or forged signatures usually have a much slower rhythm than the original, and the tracing is frequently of an identical signature – no two signatures are one hundred per cent identical even when authentic.

A writer with a high IQ can easily imitate low form level handwriting, but it is impossible for low form level writers to imitate high form level handwriting with any real success. Both forgers and anonymous letter writers are apt to forget, when trying to assume the handwriting of someone else, to suppress their own individual style of handwriting.

In fact, the really successful copying of another person's handwriting demands extraordinary skill, concentration and observation.

Illegibility

When combined with a reclining left slant, this handwriting indicates a sign of dishonesty, also when it is accompanied by open 'o's and 'a's at the base, or mixing up the same letters omitting letters and unsteady pressure. This applies only when at least four of these traits are in evidence. Unreliability is indicated by complicated starting and ending strokes, as well as the frequent use of starts of an initial stroke, and broken letters.

Figures

When figures have been altered, or forged, they are often made in the form of two or more strokes, instead of one simple direct stroke. Again re-touching will occur, and if the bottom of the oval digits are left open, this is also a sign of deceit. Clumsily written (often illegible) figures, or broad figures made with a flourish, are also signs that the writer's honesty is in question.

9   Mental Disturbances

Persecution complex: Shows itself in handwriting that has a large left margin which widens as it goes down the page. Example 123 shows how the feeling of being trapped and persecuted causes the writer to move further and further to the right, and his margin gets wider and wider. This is an extreme case.

The script is also rising upwards at a sharp angle which indicates undue optimism; the writing is, however, small and reveals intelligence. The small spacing between words shows the writer needs to be with people.

Example 123   Persecution complex

The capital 'I' is a single downstroke showing that the writer does not waste time and can pick up essentials quickly. Unfortunately his mental conflict is inhibiting his potential and he needs to ease up on the considerable tension he is under at the time of writing.

Fear of loneliness: This writer has an almost pathological fear of being on her own. Her words are jumbled without any space between them and the low level script indicates a lack of objective thinking. This writer is unable to plan or think ahead before action, and will make hasty judgments. She needs human contact so badly that she will go to extremes to get it because of her feeling of insecurity. (See Example 124.)

The setting for the play is the wide vera roofed verandah, enclosed by a rail sides of the somewhat dilapidated, tr

Example 124   Fear of loneliness

Fear of contact: This sample of writing demonstrates a reserved and proud nature. The huge gaps between words and lines, illustrate how this writer seeks to keep other people, and the world, at bay. There is a strong sense of justice in this script, and also extravagance, a love of luxury and some affectation. (See Example 125.)

Would   you   please

my   hand writing   for

purposes .

Example 125   Fear of contact

Insanity: This writer has been certified insane and the large wavy upper loops to the letters show how he has lost touch with reality.

The sharp pointed strokes are a sign of aggression, while the entire script slants dangerously to the left, indicating an introverted nature, and a severe mental disorder is revealed in this extraordinary writing with its oddly shaped formations. (See Example 126.)

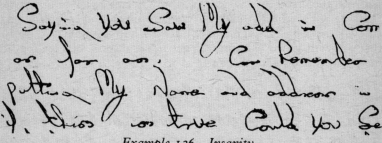

Example 126   Insanity

Religious mania: This sample shows religious mania, carried to extremes. The writer has the sign of the cross showing – a religious symbol in handwriting – and it stands out clearly from the rest of the script. The writing is abnormally large and reveals the egoism and lack of balance in the writer's personality structure. The pressure is quite heavy and the unconnected writing displays the writer's unco-operative attitude and unwillingness to conform. (See Example 127.)

Lack of emotional control: In this sample we have a clear specimen of writing showing a complete lack of emotional control. The writer is going to be excitable, impatient, reckless and almost hysterical in his pursuits. He has a dependency on outside influences and environment that is almost obsessional.

The pressure indicates that he will also suffer from nervous exhaustion and changing moods. (See Example 128.)

Hysteria: This threadlike script with its snake-like strokes, reveals manipulating powers, and the small 'o's are open at the base – a sign of dishonesty. A lack of stability and vacillation shows here. There is low resistance to outside influences, bordering on hysteria. (See Example 129.)

THAT DEVIL WHICH F
UNLOOKED FOR MO
LISTENING TO YOU I
ACCOMPLISHED A U
FOR ———— THE POIN
IT ALL STOOD PL
DETECT IN YOU, INT
NO EQUIPMENT FOI
AND RECIEVING WI
BEANTIFUL + CARE
AS ONCE, IN MY DE
PROMISED. ALAT

Example 127 Religious mania

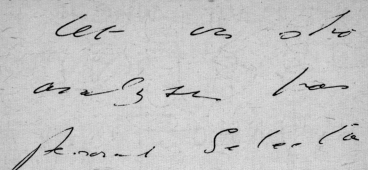

Example 128   Lack of emotional control

Example 129   Hysteria

Obsessional neurosis: This writer has a compulsive urge to keep to set patterns, and this rigid formation of script indicates that she is keeping her emotions in check to an abnormal degree. (See Example 130.)

Example 130   Obsessional Neurosis

10   Personnel Selection

Graphology can help find the right man for the job by revealing weaknesses and strengths, mental capacity, emotional stability, and intellectual and social attitudes. It can show motivation, financial sense, egoism, honesty, integrity and stability.

It can help eliminate misfits and round pegs in square holes, in indicating sexual or mental deviations, criminal tendencies, anti-social behaviour or aggressiveness, whether a man can take orders or give them, how he deals with responsibility, whether he will crack under stress or tension, cope in a crisis, is physically fit, adaptable to circumstances, mentally stable, an alcoholic or on drugs. Is his tolerance level high or low? Is he sociable and able to communicate? All these questions and many more can be answered in a graphologist's report.

The traits that most employers seek are:

> Reliability
> Integrity
> Honesty
> A capacity for developing
> Organising ability
> Ability to work with others
> Initiative
> Tenacity
> Energy and drive
> Ambition
> Leadership qualities

Obviously different kinds of work require different qualities and abilities, but this is a good example of graphology in practice.

Vocational Guidance

A field where graphology can be extremely helpful is in vocational guidance, particularly in advising young people in their choice of career.

By assessing the capabilities, potentialities, and inclinations, it is possible to steer the writer into, or away from, an expressed preference. If, for example, a youth or girl is ambitious to become a writer or play in a band, and the writing shows artistic or creative talent, then he or she may be on the right lines. But other considerations must be taken into account, such as determination, ambition, an ability to work hard, and aptitude, to mention but four.

Many people these days are tired of the rat race or working for someone else, or feel they are misfits. There is a hard core of individuals of both sexes between the ages of thirty-five and fifty, who seek the help of a graphologist in solving this problem. They want to know if they are likely to make a success of any talent they may have, however small, if they are capable of taking on new independence by starting their own business. Students also sometimes seek to change from the arts to science or vice versa.

The experienced graphologist is able to present a clear picture to the writer, revealing his weaknesses and strengths, talent or lack of it, so that he can make up his mind to take the plunge or remain where he is and strive for better things within his present environment.

This is a specialised branch of graphology and it is not possible in this book to go into more detail.

11 Marriage Compatibility

When a couple contemplating marriage seek a graphologist's report there are four important considerations to take into account. They need not necessarily be taken in this order, but they relate to the:

1 Sexual/erotic
2 Emotional
3 Social
4 Intellectual

All four are vital in differing degrees if a relationship is to be both sustained and successful, but if there is any discrepancy in one or more of these four areas, the partnership will eventually show signs of conflict.

The five most desirable aspects to look for (apart from the sexual/emotional spheres) are as follows:

1 Kindness
2 Sincerity
3 Sense of humour
4 Generosity
5 Sense of responsibility

The traits most generally disliked in marriage are:

1 Thrift
2 Dullness
3 Unreliability
4 Lack of sympathy
5 Untruthfulness

The underlengths of the writer's small 'g' and 'y' will give away his or her sexual preferences and reveal an active or passive sexual role.

A writer using long loops is not going to be compatible with a writer who has small neglected or weak underlengths to the 'g' or 'y'.

A writer with a left slant who is introverted is not going to be compatible with a writer who has a slant very much to the right and is a sociable individual.

A writer of large script who is egoistical with a need to show off, is hardly likely to have much in common with the small script writer who may be suffering from an inferiority complex or is living on higher mental plane.

The male writer who shows signs of femininity is not a good partner for a very feminine woman who seeks a partner who will dominate in a masculine way.

If two people contemplating marriage or a partnership show a marked difference in their scripts, there could be friction; a small difference makes for a more interesting relationship.

A left slanted writer is going to be introverted, a right slanted writer extroverted. These two do not make particularly good companions unless there is a degree of give and take; usually it is the social angle that causes problems, one being outward going and enjoying company, the other seeking solitude and a quiet reflective life.

A large writer and a small writer may find it difficult to establish a really satisfactory relationship because the large script is a sign of a gregarious nature, generous and friendly with a need to show off a little, and often an inflated ego, a love of physical activity and self-centredness, while a small script is a sign of a thinking person who prefers to place emphasis on the mental rather than physical aspect of life.

Thick heavy pressure with pasty strokes shows the sensualist, who enjoys eating, drinking and sex. Light carefully sustained pressure indicates the hyper-sensitive and easily hurt person and these two would obviously rub each other up the wrong way.

When two extremes are attracted to each other, as they frequently are, they are rarely of the same type. Two types of anti-social people who have angular script, spiky strokes, possibly upright writing with tiny hooks, may come together happily, but not if both are aggressive and demanding. Two highly emotional people can live happily together. This is shown by large rounded writing, with a right slant and full upper loops. But they succeed only if both are able to stand the stresses and strains of everyday living with its outbursts and tensions, which either partner generates when emotionally upset or under stress.

Weak personalities – shown by thin and weak 't' bar crossing, small capital 'I', neglected underlengths to 'g' and 'y' – are often drawn to strong personalities and the partnership may work, each giving the other support and encouragement.

A masculine man, shown by dominant pressure, looped and well balanced underlengths, firm 't' bar and slight right slanted or upright script, may choose a very feminine woman, indicated by light pressure, rounded middle zone and full loops with a right slant.

Impotence is shown in writing by weak underlengths and poor pressure. Such a writer is hardly likely to make a go of a marriage with a highly sexed woman as evidenced by a decided right slant, long looped underlengths and firm pressure.

The hypochondriac and the physical fitness fanatic are also bad bets for a partnership.

A highly intelligent man and a less intelligent woman may stand the test of time for a while but the writer with small quick fluent script will soon tire of the partner with larger script, revealing a more emotional and feeling personality and lack of mental agility.

The writer who has large embellished capitals is an egoist and should he match up with a woman with small under-developed capitals, revealing an inferiority complex, his ego could swamp her. The rounded writer is not going to be compatible with the angular writer; one being highly emotional, while the other uses head control. There would be conflict between the head and heart.

Triangular loops to 'g' and 'y' may be found in both partners' script, but the female who shows this graphic sign of disappointment is likely to assume a bossy, dominant role through her frustration, while the male will possibly turn inwards and become irritable and touchy.

Similarities in specimens of handwriting for compatibility analysis, if too alike, may possibly result in boredom and dullness.

Example 131

Example 131

This upper looped writer with her right slant and light pressure shows an emotionally impressionable nature and the connected script indicates that she needs to live and work with people. She is socially able to mix and communicate.

Example 132

Example 132

She would not be compatible with the left slant, heavier pressured and narrow script writer who crams his letters and words together showing inhibition and repression. His underlengths all swing to the left indicating his self-awareness, inward and withdrawn personality and selfishness.

Examples 133 and 134

This really high form level script writer with the thread strokes shows speed, quick thinking, versatility and a fluent mind, mental agility and good concentration – see the long downstrokes to the 'g' and 'y'. He would hardly be suitable as a partner for the rather apologetic small script of Example 134 with its almost non-existent size, large spacing between words and large margins reveal-

Thanks for the

night at the

Example 133

ing a certain amount of apprehension about the world and people.
Socially these two would be poles apart, as well as emotionally and
sexually incompatible.

For the really formal ball, choose a

taffeta backless dress trimmed with

glimmering diamante, and with frilled

Example 134

Examples 135 and 136

I love you — and miss

see if we can make

next Friday?

Example 135

This writer is energetic and physically active – long looped and rounded underlengths to her 'g' and 'y', good pressure and right slanted script – she would not make a 'go' of a relationship with Example 136 who has tiny, neglected 'g's and 'y's and displays all the symptoms of impotence in the inhibited and weak underlengths. Sexual encounters would make them both realise this very soon.

g y

Example 136

Examples 137 and 138

A Happy Birthday and looking forward to the

Example 137

Example 137 with its left slant and slightly copybook formation shows a shy, reserved person who doesn't like being in the limelight and those large spaces between words are a sign of discrimination in his choice of friends.

of any age, could take A. h help of the National Exten

Example 138

Example 138 would be the complete opposite and these two would have difficulty in establishing a rapport. He is outward going, small spaces between words showing his need for people and the outside world and its stimulation: emotionally they are at extremes.

Tony (Example 139) and Jean (Example 140)

Tony has a decided left slant, his writing is thin, narrow and reflects a lack of emotion. Jean, on the other hand, has large

Example 139   Tony

capitals and a right slant indicating her outward-going and sociable nature. These two would clash emotionally because of Tony's hyper-sensitivity and Jean's brash, almost frantic, responses to outside stimuli.

The compressed writing that Tony demonstrates shows his inhibition and repression – particularly emotional repression – while the thread-like strokes inside Jean's writing are a sign of her manipulating powers and ability to get on with people through her knowledge of them; the thread writer is nearly always able to use psychological talent to deal with people.

These two people would probably not be compatible in a marriage, but it is possible that Jean would be able to draw out the personality that lies hidden beneath the introversion that Tony displays, and in doing so she may well tone down some of the exuberance that her writing shows.

Example 140   Jean

Kate (Example 141) and Ian (Example 142)

Example 141 Kate

Kate, with her huge capitals and broad sprawling script, would hardly be compatible with Ian who has small tidy and slightly inhibited writing with a slight left slant to it. Kate is an extrovert of the first order with rounded, emotional writing and looped upper strokes.

Ian is far more introverted and more likely to relish his own company than crowds. When we look at the underlengths of both scripts, we see the difference demonstrated in the sexual area. Ian has tiny, almost neglected underlengths to his small 'g's and 'y's (even taking into account the size of his script) and Kate has long downstrokes indicating her vitality, physical energy and strong instinctive drive.

Example 142 Ian

From an intellectual angle, they could be on a similar level, but Kate is more of a doer than a thinker, and Ian has a streak of stubbornness – see the heavy 't' bar crossings that would irritate spontaneous and impulsive Kate.

Example 143

Example 143

This large right slanted script shows the writer to be an outward-going, friendly personality.

The capitals indicate her self-assurance and the wide spacing shows a need for a certain amount of space to live and work in.

The closed 'a's and 'o's show that she is able to keep her own counsel and the rounded formation of her capital 'I' shows her sense of humour.

The width of her spacing between words shows her social discrimination.

The medium pressure shows her moderate energy. The writing shows her to be a basically non-aggressive personality.

PART SEVEN

As a Graphologist Sees Them

1 Emily Brontë

Emily Brontë had two scripts – one she used for her poems which she did not want other people to read and the other for her rare personal letters.

The minute upright writing which she used for her poetry is pasty – often the sign of a genius. (See Example 144.) The larger, right slanted, almost extroverted script in her letter to Ellen Nussey (Example 145) with its long underlengths, with their inhibited formations and left tendencies, show her sexual and emotional repression. The two samples of writing could easily be thought to be by two different people.

The large spacing between her words in the letter show her isolation and discrimination, her shyness and reserve, and her inner conflicts.

The breaks between her capital letters and small letters are a sign of her highly developed intuition, while the writing reaching to the end of the page indicates her thrift and a lack of fear about the future.

The script of the letter with its speed shows vigour, whereas we know that Emily Brontë was frail and ill for most of her life, and this is even more remarkable when we see the well made firm 't' bar crossing, indicating her tremendous willpower.

The angular strokes in her writing and the emotional right slant with its social significance – a reaching out to others – is completely alien from the personality portrait we have of this outstanding woman from contemporary writers, including her own sister, Charlotte.

Therefore, we have two graphic pen portraits – the small writing of the poems indicates a mystic and emotionally inhibited woman, without any interest in the world or the people in it. The other writing in the letter to Ellen Nussey reveals a far from cold nature and a need for involvement with the world and people.

When we look at the signature, the extended stroke to her 'B' shows enterprise, and the capital 'D' shows a strong ego, and great strength of character.

Come, walk with me,
There's only thee
To bless my spirit now.
We used to love on winter nights
To wander through the snow;
Can we not woo back old delights?
The clouds rush dark and wild
They flock with storm our mountain heights,
The same as long ago
And on the horizon rest at last
In looming masses piled;
While moonbeams flash and fly so fast
We scarce can say they smiled.

Come walk with me, come walk with me;
We were not once so few
But Death has stolen our company
As sunshine steals the dew.
He took them one by one and we
Are left the only two;
So closer would my feelings twine
Because they have no stay but mine.

"May call me not it may not be
"Is human love so true?
"Can friendship's flower droop on for years
"And then revive anew?
"No, though the soil be wet with tears
"How fair soe'er it grew
"The vital sap once perished
"Will never flow again
"And surer than that dwelling dread,
"The narrow dungeon of the Dead,
"Time parts the hearts of men."

Example 144 Emily Brontë minute upright script

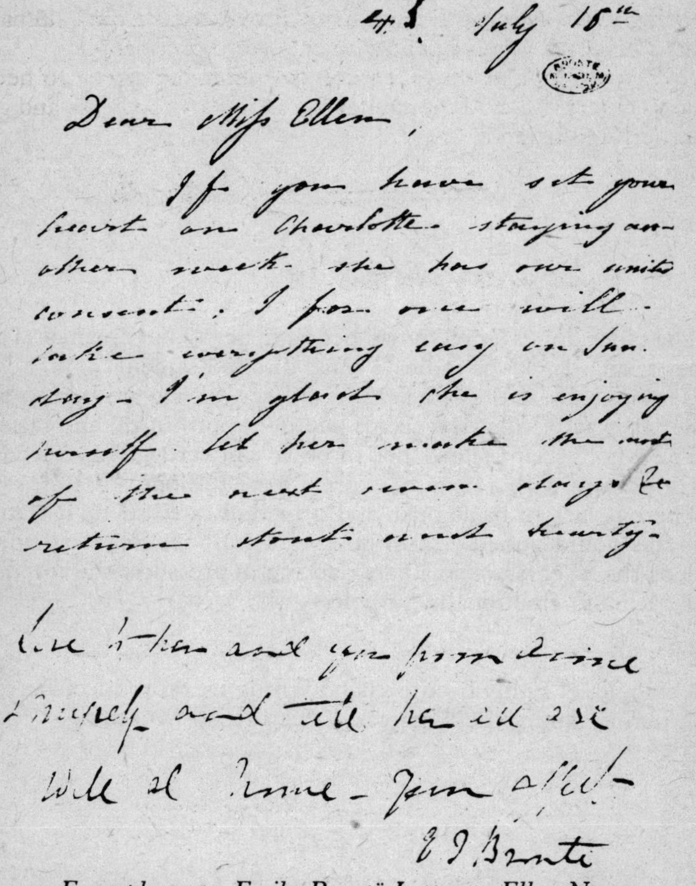

[handwritten letter]

Example 145 Emily Brontë Letter to Ellen Nussey

Example 146

This light pressured and right slanted script shows a non-aggressive personality with a liking for sociability and the rounded capital 'I' reveals her sense of humour.

The spacing is good and she could obviously organise – not at executive level, but in the home or domestic and family area – very well.

to   London   with you

times   of   Trains.

Kay

Example 146

The taller upper loops shown her tendency to daydream and the lower triangular loops indicate some disappointment.

Her signature is the same size as the rest of her writing, so this writer is exactly what she seems and does not put up any façade.

The whole script shows her to be an outward-going, friendly, warm person, with a need to express her emotions.

There is lack of basic push and drive indicated, demonstrating that she would possibly take the line of least resistance at times, and, as the 't' bars are small and lacking in pressure, she could be easily led and emotionally gullible.

The samples of Emily Brontë's handwriting are reproduced here by kind permission of the Trustees of the British Museum.

Bibliography

Hearns, Rudolph S., *Handwriting: An Analysis Through its Symbolism*, Vantage Press, 1966.

Jacoby, H. J., *Analysis of Handwriting*, George Allen & Unwin, 1939.

Marcuse, Irene, *Applied Graphology*, Macoy Publishing Co., 1946.

Mendel, Alfred O., *Personality in Handwriting*, Stephen Daye Press, 1947.

Roman, K. G., *Handwriting, A Key to Personality*, Routledge & Kegan Paul, 1954.

Saudek, Robert, *The Psychology of Handwriting*, George Allen & Unwin, 1925.

Singer, Eric, *A Manual of Graphology*, Duckworth, 1969.

Sonnemann, Urich, *Handwriting Analysis*, Grune & Stratton, 1950.

Index